MIKE BULL

AN OLYMPIAN'S STORY

DR. MICHAEL BULL O.B.E

BALLYHAY BOOKS

First published by Ballyhay Books,
An imprint of Laurel Cottage Ltd.
Ballyhay, Donaghadee, N. Ireland 2021.
Copyrights Reserved.
© Text Dr Michael Bull.
Photographs Dr Michael Bull private collection unless otherwise annotated.
Cover photo courtesy of Mark Shearman MBE
All rights reserved.
No part of this book may be reproduced or stored on any media
without the express written permission of the publishers.
Design & origination Laurel Cottage Ltd.
Printed & bound by GPS Colour Graphics Ltd
ISBN 978 1910657 15 7

Dedicated to
Chief Petty Officer F.W.J. Bull, BA (QUB)

FOREWORD BY LYNN DAVIES

OLYMPIC LONG JUMP GOLD MEDAL WINNER TOKYO 1964

For anyone with even the slightest interest in sport, this is a great story which needs to be told. The story of the journey of a young sportsman in Northern Ireland, growing up in troubled and challenging times who, despite the odds, achieved his dreams of becoming an Olympian.

It is all the more enjoyable because I travelled with him on much of the journey including visits to Northern Ireland where we trained together, staying at his home, meeting up with his Mum and Dad and wife Christina, competing against him in Paisley Park, and in later years charity golf days and walks to support him in his role as Chairman of Sparks.

We travelled together on many occasions, Great Britain matches, Commonwealth, European and Olympic Games when, sharing rooms together and between training sessions he would enlighten me on the thoughts of the great philosophers, Aristotle and Plato, having himself graduated from Queens with a Doctorate in the subject.

He left academia though and opened the Mike Bull gym which became a great inspirational centre for aspiring young sportsmen and women as well as being a great motivator for those seeking health and fitness just like Buster McShane before him.

He describes how I inspired him to follow his dream when as a young athlete he saw me training for the Tokyo Olympic Games of 1964. Little did we realise then that a great friendship would follow which continues to this day, and thanks to visiting him on a holiday, in southern Spain about 20 years ago me and my wife Meriel discovered La Cala and we now spend many holidays there together. So the journey continues!

Mike is a sporting legend in Northern Ireland and his story demonstrates what can be achieved with great desire and perseverance.

Thanks for the memories Mike. Great book.

Gestation

The only thing that I know is that I know nothing.

– Socrates

Socrates was certainly right when it comes to publishing, I knew absolutely nothing about it. The bare bones of this story were initially written by 2003, but my clumsy attempts to get it published led to the sole copy of the manually typed script going missing until my daughter Natalie, through Herculean efforts, managed to find it again. She presented it in the original crumpled plastic bag at Christmas 2017, much to my surprise and delight.

Life had moved on apace since the original writing, meaning a lot of new stories to be told in the light of twenty-odd intervening years of experience. Let's hope that Oscar Wilde was wrong when he said "experience… was merely the name men gave to their mistakes", because this publishing hiatus created a period of gestation for me to refine and, hopefully, improve the original manuscript. If the definition of gestation is 'conception and development in the mind', then I can at least tick that box now. I realize that the current vogue is for sports stars to produce 'life stories' almost as soon as they step off the rostrum, but there would seem to be a certain truth in the saying about the improvement of fine wine with age. The proof of this will be in the reading. I hope you get some enjoyment out of it.

Michael Bull

CONTENTS

1. THE PIVOTAL MOMENT

The sky above Kingston, Jamaica, was inky black. From my worm's eye view a billion stars peppered the canopy. It was the evening of the closing ceremony of the 1966 Commonwealth Games and the band had struck up a rousing march for the entrance into the national stadium of all the teams in orderly lineup behind their countries' flags. More like disorderly, as you've often seen before, youthful exuberance bursting into dancing and prancing, piggyback rides all over the place as all the nations break ranks in spontaneous expression of joy and relief. Sporting youth in unconstrained celebration.

A mere spectator to all of this, I was lying on top of the pole vault landing area, actually a pile of sacks stuffed with hay because it was 1966 and compressed foam rubber beds hadn't reached the Caribbean yet (indeed they hadn't even reached the British Isles!).

At the Commonwealth games in Kingston
Photo: Belfast Telegraph archive

Everyone has a moment in time, a formative experience in life and this was mine.

Call it life-changing, a game changer or whatever, but I like the word 'pivotal', defined as 'vitally important' or 'crucial', conjuring up the idea that things could have gone a different way, something teetering on the axis of success and failure. This was my pivotal moment in sport. Let me explain.

THE PIVOT

I was sitting in the vault pit in some sort of trance, with a silly grin on my face, thinking of what had happened a few minutes ago. The pole vault had been the very last event of the Games, finishing late in the evening after a titanic jump-off between myself and the Australian champion. The medal ceremony was held immediately after, which explains why I wasn't in line for the closing ceremony. I had won a surprise silver medal for the NI team, 3 inches behind the great Australian Trevor Bickle but breaking with him the Commonwealth record and setting my first UK record at 15ft 6in (4.75m).

The medal was now hanging proudly around my neck. At 19 and a 2nd year student at Queen's University Belfast, I was British record holder and new number one. But it all could have been so different.

I had opted to start jumping at a safe 14ft (4.30m), safe because all season I had been clearing 15ft (4.60m) and had improved the Irish record up to 15ft 2in (4.63m). But here I was at the end of the runway, my knees knocking and legs feeling like jelly. I had hit the bar off twice and now it was my third and final attempt.

This had happened to me before in minor events but this was serious business, my first big international games. I was no novice, having made rapid progress in the previous 3 years since learning to vault at St Malachy's College Belfast. In 1964 I had set British junior records while a sports scholarship student at Southern Illinois University, Irish and NI senior records and, aged 18 in 1965 had become a full GB International. So there was no need to panic... except I was panicking and that crossbar set at 14ft looked awful high, that runway in the

Kingston national stadium felt a very lonely place. It was no place for faint hearts.

I was thinking of all that hard training over the past 3 years, the very real sacrifices my parents had made, letting down my team mates in the NI squad and all the sport's followers at home, the local press hyping up my prospects. I was thinking of every clichéd sentiment you have ever heard of as I prepared for the third and final attempt.

My brain was undergoing what sports psychologists nowadays call an 'Amygdala Hijack', where the primitive 'fight, flight or freeze' response has been activated by a small, almond-shaped mass of brain cells, the amygdala. The sheer terror of my impending failure was raising my heart rate, already racing with an adrenaline surge making my heart palpitate against my vest – not that I understood any of this at the time, my first year psychology at Queens had covered frightening events like lion attacks, but not opening height third attempts at major championships!

I recall trying to take breaths to calm my racing heart. I mentally rehearsed a couple of basic, key points of technique like 'get the pole up high at take off' and 'press the lower arm hard against the pole'. The effect of these reasoning nanoseconds, unknown to me at the time, was to moderate the Amygdala Hijack and allow the athlete, me, to utilise the heightened physical state to execute my ingrained jumping ability. Almost like going on automatic pilot.

ENTER THE ZONE

The effect was dramatic. I cleared the bar by a mile and thereby made my entry into the Games. I also entered the 'zone'.

There were to be no more mistakes, no more knocking the bar down, and no more knocking of knees for me at this event. My mind and body had entered what many sports champions today call 'the zone' and what modern psychologists refer to as 'flow'. In the flow state sports persons reach the zenith of concentration and focus on the task at hand, where all sense of time can be lost and where formerly impossible actions can become effortless. It does not happen often to elite athletes, maybe only a few times in a whole career, but invariably the stakes are high and the prize important. It was to happen to me in a few future crucial championships as you will soon learn.

In my case, the near disaster of travelling halfway round the world to fail ignominiously at the lowly opening height in my first Games had shocked me into the athletic zone of peak performance. In this state I went on to clear 14ft 6in (4.45m), 15ft (4.60m), 15ft 3in (4.65m) and 15ft 6in (4.75m) all on the first attempt, to lead the competition and win the silver medal, only eventually finding 15ft 9in (4.80m) and the gold beyond my reach.

My life's direction was fixed at this point by my success. But what if I hadn't made that 3rd attempt at 14ft? For a start, I would not have had the acclaim at home normally reserved for sports persons with a ball, Ulster sportsman of the year and all-Ireland Texaco award. The sporting pathway was now clearer. My UK record was above the qualifying standard for the European Championships to be held in Budapest in two weeks time and I was added to the British team.

I performed well in Budapest, reaching the final and my status as the country's number one was enhanced by selection for two more GB internationals later in the season. So began a record unbroken run of 69 GB Internationals over the next ten years.

However, the single most important result of all this was that I was now being considered a serious contender for a place on the GB Olympic team. The Mexico Olympics were less than two years away and the vault qualifying standard of 15ft 9in (4.80m) was well within reach.

Although regular top level competition across Europe was to be squeezed in between university studies, the spoils of war were now lining up: free equipment and sports wear, trainers and spikes, and the all-important vaulting poles from the US manufacturers.

The die had been cast. The Commonwealth Games silver was the turning point for sure. However, it was not strictly speaking the beginning. That had been almost 20 years earlier on the eleventh of September 1946.

2. NINE-ELEVEN

The eleventh of September, nine/eleven in American-speak, is portentous enough a date for a birth, mine, but in 1946 all the omens were good for the immediate post-war generation of baby-boomers. The war was over and my father John, a Royal Navy chief petty officer, found himself stationed at Eglington, near Londonderry, in the role of physical training instructor. He had met and married my mother, Anne, a Belfast hairdresser and a

Mini me at six months at Eglington Naval Base

war widow with three young children who had been surviving alone since her army Paratrooper husband had been killed in action, early in the war.

John Bull was himself as English as his name, born in Bristol into a seafaring family with a Royal Navy father and roots in Britain's maritime expansion, going back to the time of Captain Cook. John's father, my grandfather, whom neither I nor my father ever knew, had been knocked off his bicycle and killed in an accident with a charabanc at Weston-Super-Mare when my father was less than a year old. I have always wondered just how many traffic accidents there were in Weston-Super-Mare in 1920?

JOHN BULL

My father John Bull, ready for war at 18 years of age

Despite the crushing poverty suffered by many in the 1920s including John's mother and stepfather, John became a sporting prodigy at school and could never seem to eat enough food to fill his huge frame to fuel his relentless physical pursuits. At 14 years he was just over six feet tall weighing in at a muscular 14 stone and was a natural, if involuntary, boxer who stopped the school bully in the ring in a bout arranged by the headmaster to settle a playground confrontation. However his main sports were athletics, with a county title at 200m, and soccer, where he was already being sought by Bristol Rovers Football Club as an outstanding young goalkeeper.

The austerity at his stepfather's home, where food and lodging had to be shared with stepbrothers and sister, turned the young John Bull's thoughts and dreams to the idea of a life at sea in the Royal Navy. In 1936 he duly enlisted at the age of 15. It is not certain how John managed to convince the authorities he was the correct age to enlist, but size and strength were not an issue.

Thus began a fighting man's war and a 12-year educational tour of duty, which would see John decorated and mentioned in war theatres from the North Atlantic and Mediterranean to Russia. Sport was fitted in at quieter ports of call when the man had grown fully to 6ft 1in and weighed 16 stone, big enough to be pressed to enter the highly prestigious Inter-Services heavyweight boxing championship, which he duly won.

WHEN YOUR FATHER'S NAME IS JOHN BULL

In 1966 I came back from Kingston, Jamaica with a Commonwealth Games silver medal and a new UK National Record of 15ft 6ins, my first of 25 such records. I was 19 and was greeted with a newspaper headline to an article by Bill Rutherford, a legendary Ulster journalist who assiduously fostered my career throughout all the trials and tribulations; the headline said, *When Your Father's Name Is John Bull*. I guess that the sentence should continue, 'England expects', or in my case Great Britain expects.

I was raised on wonderful tales of exploding depth charges; in one instance the charge sticking to the launch pod and blowing up in the hands of a seaman and friend that my father had sent to dislodge the errant explosive, which sent his head rolling down deck, pipe still in mouth and eyes wide open. There were reminiscences of diving Luftwaffe fighters and gun battles that blazed for 30 sleepless hours, of sinking ships and being adrift in cold seas and hand-to-hand fighting behind enemy lines in North Africa, where the small crew of ship-wrecked sailors were led to safety by their only officer, my father.

My earliest recollection of sport was accompanying my father on his weekend training sessions. Riding high on his shoulders, along with a training bag containing a 16-pound throwing hammer, I would insist on being carried up the stairs of the double-decker bus. There were also the rugby matches and training sessions at the famous North Club and at the YMCA, where my father was the 1st XV captain.

The changing area at this club had a room with a barbell and some home-made weights and I would do make-believe workouts there when the players were out on the pitch playing. My father had some stalwarts in the team, including a mercurial little man called Eddie who would really pound the iron weights. I can still remember the pungent mixture of sweat and Elliman's liniment wafting in the air of that dressing room. The somewhat Spartan facilities, compared with present day state of the art provision, remind me of how sportsmen had to improvise in those days. I can still remember the 'shower' was a large hooped barrel full of rainwater at the side of the club room and that necessary ability to make use of whatever you could lay your hands on was to stand me in good stead. I found myself many years later using that skill of improvisation when I was designing landing pits made of foam mattresses for my pole-vaulting activities, using raw materials available in the shipyard. Indeed,

I was to make good use of the shipyard workers as well and that is another story for a future chapter.

Looking back on those early activities and recalling the smells of the freshly cut grass and not so fresh changing room, there is no doubt that such exposure to sportsmen left a formative mark on me. I wanted to excel in sport and emulate some of the excellent sportsmen I saw around me, coached and trained by my father. I simply soaked up the camaraderie among the players. Already sport was dripping into my blood.

When recalling memories of early sporting activities, I, in common with lots of other people, find the smell of newly mown grass conjures up images of freshly prepared sports grounds ready for matches and other exciting contests. School sports days still reawaken long forgotten memories of distant events and competitions, and victories. This was the genesis of a very powerful drug, sporting success and peer adulation.

My home in North Belfast was full of sporting magazines, which were popular in that era, with titles like *The Ring*, *World Sport* and *Health and Strength*. There was also a huge punch bag hanging from the attic door and these enormous old brown leather boxing gloves, which would engulf my whole arm. In this environment I was taught the science of self-defence and the art of daydreaming about sporting fame.

My father had taught me to swim when I was five years old and, under the guidance of local swimming and water polo legends Ronnie Flude, Eddie Skelly and Fred Parks at the Wellington Club, based at Belfast's Ormeau Baths, I built up strength and stamina in the pool. I was also continually sneaking into the little glory hole at the foot of the stairs of our Housing Trust house in Sunninghill Drive, in North Belfast, to play with my father's weightlifting equipment – this before the age of eleven!

Given this early exposure to sport and physical education in my life, the young Mike, or Mickey, as I was known at St Malachy's College Grammar School in Belfast, was one of the physically fittest ten-year old's to come through the gates of that prestigious school.

The scene was set for academic and sporting achievement but, of course, as with most things in life, it is never quite that straightforward.

3. GLORIA AB INTUS - SCHOOL

St Malachy's College, gateway to glory
Photo; courtesy Bronagh Goudy

The school motto *Gloria Ab Intus* at St Malachy's College Belfast means 'glory from within', but any plans of glory, either within or without, that my parents may have made for their son certainly were not shared by me. What is that old saying? 'Have a five-year plan and make God smile'.

If my parents had any sort of master plan for me at school my mother would have been hoping for me to enter the priesthood while my father would have settled for anything to do with sport. One of them was going to be disappointed.

At the outset nothing really looked promising for me at this famous educational institution, established in 1833, which historically prided itself on producing two types of human being, namely priests and scholars. The list of celebrated alumni includes Sir Charles Russell, 19th century Lord Chief Justice of England; Cardinal Daly, Primate of All Ireland; Bernard MacLaverty, writer of novel and movie, *Cal*; Eamonn

Holmes OBE, broadcaster; and Martin O'Neill OBE, football player and manager; and innumerable celebrated clerics, lawyers, medics and politicians.

My aptitude for the priesthood was rendered doubtful, both by an inability to learn a single Latin phrase, despite five years of class, and an early appreciation of the fairer sex; at any rate, I did not even make altar boy.

As for scholarship, well, I must have been hiding my light under several bushels. If truth be told, my lowly placing on the end of term lists must have placed my very survival at the College at risk.

I had one saving grace; I was good at Physical Education. The problem was that this school was, in 1957, seriously academic and although sport and physical education enjoyed a great tradition, they were only important in so far as they contributed to the really important thing in life… passing exams!

There was another problem, more complicated and all-pervasive. I was painfully self-conscious, bordering on having an inferiority complex, and this was to remain with me, heavily disguised, throughout the rest of my career.

THE EARLY YEARS

Feelings of inferiority are common among adolescents. However, with my size and physical aptitude one could be forgiven for expecting such a boy to immediately shine in a competitive environment. Perhaps it was this burden of expectation that weighed too heavily, because I did not exactly set the world alight. Nothing pathological you understand, not like that great sports writing, speaking and running Doctor, George Sheehan's depiction of the neurotic athlete who always averts eye-contact, keeps his head down and says nothing (see his *Running and Being*). But fairly tightly wrapped up all the same.

My father was a well-known Physical Education teacher at both Belfast High School and Grosvenor Grammar School. He was, quite literally, a larger than life figure who, although not a particularly extroverted personality, possessed a wonderfully resonant, booming English voice. This was used to good effect at school sports grounds and in rugby refereeing all over the North. It was also used on the stage. In the early fifties the name John Bull had become well known as a very popular baritone singer and I have fond memories of going with my mother to see dad perform at Belfast's Empire Theatre, with Joseph Locke topping the bill, (the hard-living but magnetic Locke was my mother's favourite, much to father's irritation).

The point is I was growing up under the shadow of this giant of a man, war hero, all-round sportsman, teacher and opera singer. What child could hope to shine in such a bright firmament?

BAD FAITH AND PUNISHMENT

I was always very self-conscious. Deep embarrassment would be provoked by the slightest scrutiny, by what Sartre has termed 'the regard of others'. According to the French philosopher in his seminal work, *Being and Nothingness*, this over-sensitivity in the presence of other, equally frail, mortals is the source of man's bad faith, or *'mauvaise foi'* as he called it. In my own case it was just that I turned bright red at the slightest hint of embarrassment. The trouble was that almost every classroom lesson offered the opportunity to demonstrate one's ignorance and, in consequence, produce the dreaded crimson tide. Sport was to change all that; no room for bad faith in the arena! Or for blushing!

CANED AND ABLE

There was also the strong possibility of getting the cane. Our Latin master, with long graduate's gown worn like body armour, thick black helmet-like hair and trusty hand-held bamboo cane as his 'gladius', would punish pupils' every mistake with the mantra, "Stand out!". This meant standing at the front of the classroom waiting to be whacked on the palm of the hand at the end of the lesson, usually in the company of most of the class.

The crook-like length of bamboo was the teachers' instrument and weapon of choice, the rod of discipline which ruled over one and a half thousand boisterous boys. It was used to expurgate all manner of indiscretions, from the morning late-comers who had to line up, often in front of their parents, after just missing the last clang of the hand-bell, to those caught running in the corridors or, least justifiably of all, for getting a math's equation or language translation wrong.

It was a rule of fear; but it worked. There was definitely no back-chatting the Dracula-like, black-gowned tyrants who taught at this venerable establishment under the auspices of the Christian Brothers, (whom the late, great broadcaster and philosopher, Gerry Anderson, jokingly called "the paramilitary wing of the Catholic Church"). And if, per chance, some unfortunate soul did appear to be crossing the line of authority there was always the ultimate religious sanction. As Bob Dylan put it, "…with God on their side."

SWIMMING

In spite of all this, it was at St Malachy's that I first made my mark in sport. I felt at ease with most physical activities, but swimming was my forte. At the annual School Gala, held in the Falls Road Baths, I regularly won five or six championships and set long standing freestyle sprint records. Irish swim and water polo champion, Jim Hurson, and coach at our swim club, Clonard, Con O'Callaghan, told me I was sure to be an Irish swimming champion. Dangerous talk for a day-dream believer like me!

There was a measure of justice in this success since, in order to train at the Baths, I had to cross the loyalist Shankill Road on foot. Most days after school, getting to a swim session involved running along the narrow, tenement-house streets of the area wearing the distinctive Malachy's uniform. This often involved running a gauntlet of abuse and taunts from the gangs of corner boys that invariably congregated after school hours (which I am sure was reciprocated when the roles were reversed). Nothing nasty ever happened but the sense of hostility and fear was real enough for any vulnerable young person on forbidden turf. I would pull up the collar of my school blazer to conceal the tell-tale green and black tie and run like hell the two miles distance to the pool. I became an excellent runner!

My swimming ambitions took a serious hit when I was about 15. Invited to race in an international 100ms freestyle at the Grove Pool. I lined up on the block and reacted to the start whistle in what I thought was a pretty fast dive. However, as I leaped forward, in mid-air I saw out of the corner of my eye the kicking heels of the swimmer in the next lane already on his way up the first length of the pool! He won in a near world record time of 54secs; his name was Bobby McGregor, a scot who was soon to become Olympic silver medallist in Tokyo in 1964. Struggling some way behind, I resolved there and then to stick to athletics. Bobby was to be a team-mate of mine on the GB World Student Games squad some years later. We had a laugh about that Grove event.

It would be a mistake to underestimate the simmering politico-religious friction that permeated life in pre-troubles Belfast, given the horrors that were to come. It was difficult to ignore this tension between the two rival politico-religious factions, and there can be little doubt that my own feelings of inferiority were nourished by the accident of birth that made me a member of 'the minority'. Nevertheless, in spite of the strident indoctrination at school and the God-fearing principles of my parents, I managed to eschew religion in my mid- teens. Eventually the opportunity to travel the world in pursuit of my chosen sport, and to open my mind to other cultures, liberated me, to some extent, from the politico-religious morass. I had decided that my religion was going to be 'Sport', and that my politics were going to be 'Olympism'.

4. Early Heroes

To return to the main theme; when I was 12 my father, whether because he saw some potential or just wanted to keep me from pinching his weights from under the stairs, enrolled me in Buster McShane's Health Studio, an aspiring gym on the top floor of an old linen factory in Belfast's Corporation Street. Every Monday, Wednesday and Friday after school myself and my school pals, Danny Farrell, who was to be my future partner in the gym business, Gerry Conlon and Joe Clerkin would go to the gym to do weight training.

With Buster at Crystal Palace in 1972 just having set a new UK record at 5.11m

There were holes in the wooden floorboards and cracking paint and plaster on the walls and ceiling; the weight machines, such as there were, were home-made and rusting; but magic was everywhere. The growing legend of East Belfast strongman, Buster, and his dynamic wee brother, Noel, filled those pungent rooms, where old black and white photos in cracked glass frames displayed their muscular physiques and depicted fabled feats of Herculean strength.

The magic came from the brothers, both of them, so it seemed to us wee lads, five foot six in height and close to that in width, judging by the expanse of material in the shoulders of their tailored suits. They drew up our training schedules and would sit down with us and discuss our progressions each week, the dreaded ritual 'marking up' of training cards. Compared to the soul-less fitness factories of today, this shabby little room on the top floor of a drab Victorian factory block was a place where an enthusiastic young lad could be inspired; a place where you would be coached, cajoled and always encouraged by the old salts of the pioneering days of pumping iron and regaled with wonderful stories of their heroic feats. This was a very Irish gym, and the craic was always good.

Some of the stories were more than just fairy tales. Monumental events often unfolded before our highly impressionable eyes. On one occasion training was interrupted when everyone made for the windows to get a look at what seemed to be a street fight on the pavement below. Buster and Noel dropped everything and, quick as an Olympic sprinter, bounded down the stairs out onto the street making for the doorway where an older man was being beaten up by what we knew by their dress-code were 'teddy-boys,' slick-back hairstyles, sideburns, long 'frock' coats and drainpipe trousers with thick, crepe -soled suede shoes.

These three thugs were punching and kicking this defenceless old man as our action men arrived on the scene. The ensuing events played like a bar brawl in a John Wayne western; frocked coats flew through the air, their occupants anaesthetized by the heavy-duty onslaught of the mighty avengers, who reduced them to an undignified and crumpled heap on the pavement. Retributive justice was the entirely satisfactory conclusion of the terrible thrashing the 'teds' received at the hands of our heroes. From our lofty perch by the fifth-floor windows the gym members erupted in a cacophony of spontaneous applause. The legend was enshrined. I wanted to be like them.

ARTHUR ROWE

On another occasion when Danny and I were training as usual in the gym this huge Englishman arrived, purportedly to train and compete with Buster in a strength test called the 'bench press'. This is a movement in weight lifting where the bar is taken at arm's length from a position lying on your back on a bench, the bar then lowered to touch the chest and finally pushed up to arm's length again. Prodigious amounts could be achieved in this way by strong men and women (Mary Peters lifted 105kg, or 230lbs, easily during our pre-Olympic training). I myself was the talk of the gym for a while when at age 16 I cheat-benched 300lbs (135kg) and Danny, who was soon to be asked to instruct in the gym part-time (the ultimate accolade), was not far behind.

We soon learned that the big man was from Yorkshire and was the European champion in putting the shot and that he was one of the hot favourites for the Gold Medal in the forthcoming Rome Olympic Games in the summer of 1960. His name was Arthur Rowe.

Arthur Rowe was 6ft tall and about 16 and a half stone(105kg). Buster, on the other hand, was a pocket Hercules at 5ft 6in and less than 12 stone. To an untrained eye the result of their bench press challenge should have been a foregone conclusion. It wasn't. The smaller, lighter man won with a superb new world record (for his weight category) of 435lbs (198kg), with Arthur only 5lbs behind.

Some years later, in his published obituary to his friend Buster, the great Belfast journalist, Malcolm Brodie, eloquently told the story;

> 'Buster was a lean, lithe 14 year-old when he looked into the window of a store in Smithfield (Market). A pair of shining chest expanders caught his eye. But the £1 10 shillings price tag was beyond his means. The salesman saw the disappointed look on his face. He decided to compromise; "Stretch them and they're yours at half price," he said. Buster duly obliged. In that same shop he saw a course by Bob Hoffman.
>
> He bought the books for 32s 6d and paid it off at 2s 6d a week. Standing only 5ft 6in tall this stocky figure became an internationally known strength specialist. He set a world bench press record of 430lbs in 1957. Three years later he pushed it to 435lbs.'

Malcolm's dating confirms that it was 1960, the year of the Rome Olympics. Arthur Rowe would have had other things on his mind. I would have been 13 at the time and not very interested in athletics, but I do remember being immensely impressed by the quiet dignity of this mighty athlete who pushed our local hero all the way to a world record. Even then it seemed obvious to me that the long, athletic levers of the shot-putter were a distinct disadvantage in an event where the compact frame and short arms of Buster would mean that the heavy barbell would only have to travel a matter of inches, whereas Arthur appeared to be pushing up forever in order to get the bar at arm's length. A mechanical advantage, you could call it.

In any case, mechanics or not, the late, great Arthur Rowe, was added to my list of role models. I didn't simply admire him. I wanted to be just like him.

I actually met Arthur, who tragically passed away in 2003, in person in 1981 at the Sportsmen of the Century awards dinner in London. We sat at the same table and I was still like the star-struck schoolboy in the great athlete's presence. I did manage, however, to retell the story of Buster and himself all those years ago. He laughed heartily, and I did manage to get his autograph, but only on his condition that I give him mine. He had been a close follower of my sporting career over the years. And by the way, the Rome Olympics were a disaster for Arthur when he contracted a gastric bug, lost a stone in body weight and failed to qualify for the final, throwing some 10ft less than usual. He then turned professional, to rugby league. I bet he took some stopping!

REG

During these early school years my real heroes were on the big silver screen at the local cinema. At the time there was great interest in the epic Hercules movies, with bodybuilders like Steve Reeves and Reg Park displaying their massively muscular physiques in the heroic role. There was always plenty of action and incredible feats of strength, and there was always discus throwing and Greek athletes running and jumping with poles; this latter always caught my attention - it looked like fun.

One day at our usual gym training session at Buster's a notice went up on the cork board, standing out from the other ads selling dumbbells, bars and loose weights and ads offering welding services. It announced in large print,

REG PARK
AT
THE KING GEORGE V MEMORIAL HALL

In conjunction with the staging of a Junior Mr Ireland Under-16 physique contest our idol Reg, Hercules himself, was going to be the star guest poser in Belfast. Danny and I somehow had to see this but, at 5s entrance fee, it was way beyond our means, the cost of two weeks training at the gym. The only solution was to enter the Under 16 event. This would guarantee the chance to see our mythical hero. We entered the event that day. We also entered the unknown.

On stage at the Memorial Hall the MC for the evening introduced the first young contestant in the Junior Mr Ireland as, "Mickey Bull from St Malachy's College, a young man who is making a bit of a name for himself in local discus throwing and swimming".

It was a fair enough introduction. I was doing quite well as a freestyle sprinter in the pool and had represented Northern Ireland Schools where I was second fastest boy in the province to Paddy Graham of the Royal Belfast Academical Institution. We were the only boys in the province at the time who were regularly beating 60 seconds for the 100m.

I had also been winning junior competitions in the shot and discus and I had discovered that I could leap with an aluminium pole over heights that were considered prodigious in this part of the world.

Introductions complete, I clumsily performed my little posing routine and was duly rewarded with third place, the title going to the much more compact and muscular physique of my pal Danny.

We were delighted and excited in equal measure because next on stage was Reg Park, the main reason for our being there in the first place.

Reg was a master of his art. He crouched on the darkened platform, much like Arnold Schwarzeneggar in the opening scene of 'Terminator', as the stirring music of the *Theme from Exodus* struck up to exactly coincide with a spotlight hitting his right calf muscle which twitched and flexed to reveal the biggest gastrocnemius ever seen in Ireland. As the music on the crackling sound-system reached a crescendo the massive Hercules uncoiled, as if from a chrysalis, into the huge, fully extended mass of muscle and sinew that hallmarked the Mr Universe standing before our eyes.

The obligatory standing ovation was followed by Buster explaining and Reg demonstrating to an enraptured audience some of his favourite barbell exercises. As the giant played with the one hundred-pound (50kg) bar this promising young athlete was mightily impressed. I wanted to be just like him!

5. First Leaps

My first ever competitive leap with pole was in the annual St Malachy's versus St McNisi's, a winning debut at the astronomical height of 8ft. People often ask, "How did you get over the bar that first time you tried?" and "How do you actually start?" I think they see it a bit like a ski-jump, "How does someone go to the top of the 100ms hill and just fly off?" Well, of course, the answer is "he doesn't"; the novice ski-jumper will first of all learn to jump from a two- foot- high mound of snow, gradually building up over many years practice to the 100ms tower.

In a similar fashion, the pole-vaulter normally learns in progressive stages – but not in my case! Our PE teacher, Mick McCormick, a Loughborough graduate who had played basketball and water-polo at a good level and had learned the principles of vaulting, eschewed the theory of easy, progressive stages. He had his own method of initiation into the realm of gravity-defiance. He would stand at one end of the gymnasium holding an old metal pole jammed into a pile of old-style gym mats (compressed foam rubber cushions had not yet been invented). The boys of any given class would line up, petrified, at the far end and, in turn, run down and leap onto the end of the pole which Mick would then whip up to the vertical. Thereby, the human fly on the end would be propelled through the air with the greatest of ease, or, in most cases, unease. If agile enough, the boy would land and roll on the scant safety offered by the gym mats, having successfully tasted the sweet scent of adrenaline-fuelled flight or fright. The less able would slip ignominiously down the pole and land at the feet of the bellowing Mick or, worse, they would fail to release their grip and have to hold on for grim death as the pole was whisked to the vertical with the poor lads crashing, if lucky, on to the mats on the seat of their pants.

Using this do or die method Mick had secured a long line of vaulting victories at the annual Ulster Grammar School Sports, reminiscent of the great tradition of Irish pole leaping that saw one of the event's earliest recorded competitions at the ancient Tailteann Games (which were a funeral celebration of the mother of an ancient sage in 1800 BC in Co. Meath, centuries before the ancient Olympics in Greece).

Thus to return to the question about how I started vaulting, the honest answer may seem rather prosaic; nevertheless, it is true to say that the first time I jumped on to that hand-held pole in the school gymnasium it was as if this was the most natural thing in the world.

Age 17 at St Malachy's school sports in 1964. Clearing 12ft 4in with a bamboo pole into a shallow sandpit for an Irish junior record – survival optional!

It was easy for me to grip tightly because I was strong for my age and, because I was tall and quite a fast runner, I could take a much higher grip up on the pole than the rest of the boys. The result was relatively spectacular and immediately apparent to Mick; here was a lad who was able to climb higher than anyone he had seen before, much too high for those meagre gym mats to ensure any degree of safety. I was banished from the confines of the gymnasium and sent out to the sports field, where grass would at least offer softer landings than a sprung pine floor and where I might be saved from breaking my neck.

THE GLORY YEARS

When I was about fifteen I had a short spell of teenage rebellion and, in our Ballysillan Road neighbourhood in North Belfast, I ran for a while with a roistering gang of rebels-without-a-cause led by Charlie Mulholland (the oldest and by far the toughest), Doc (I don't know why so called but he often wore a flat cap and always held his cigarette butt cupped between thumb and finger behind his back, and always had a back-up tucked behind his ear), Frock (as per the long frock coat he always wore, even playing football), Blackie (hair slicked back, the apparently most affable lad but one whom nobody ever crossed because of a little matter of his facility with a switch-blade), Silver (hair), Beads (as in 'eyes like'), Mickey Coogan (who had about 8 older sisters, all beautiful), Sheriff Burt (who always dressed as a cowboy and has remained totally unchanged over the last 50 years), et al. At school I progressed unremarkably through the old Junior Certificate, unremarkably that is if you discount a close call with expulsion for truancy, fighting, a little matter of broken shop windows that the local police were investigating, bottom of the class term exam results, and general unsmiling, dumb insolence. A normal teenager in fact!

The trouble was my elders simply did not understand how hard it was trying to be just like teenage movie idol James Dean, (it may be of interest to note that Dean was a high-school state pole-vaulter). My father certainly did not have much sympathy and, after one memorable thrashing at his hands, I ran away from home for three days to my Auntie Eileen's. In hindsight, although at the time I felt I was striking a major blow for freedom the fact that Auntie Eileen was my God Mother and

Mum's best friend somewhat diluted that claim. No matter, it seemed to get it out of my system because, although I think I managed to retain a little bit of the old Jimmy Dean spirit of rebelliousness, generally speaking from that point on I kept my head down and worked away at the A-levels and sport; anything to avoid a repeat of the crashing right hand of the former Inter-Services heavyweight boxing champion.

My senior years at school reflected an improving academic record and a growing commitment to the sport of athletics. The source for the accurate chronology of my sporting career is a six-volume collection of thick, meticulously denoted scrapbooks kept by my father. They trace my story from those first swimming races as an eleven- year-old schoolboy to the more recent period of press interest in my involvement with Ulster and Ireland Rugby as their Fitness Coach. It is all in there, starting with furtive leaps into a makeshift mound of sand on the school gaelic field, where I was to set a long-standing school and Irish junior vault record of 12ft 10in (with only one inch of sand dumped on the grass to land on) at a time when the Irish men's record was only ¾in higher and the British best not too far away at 14ft 4in. This was in the spring of 1964. The previous summer, when I was only fifteen, my father had enrolled us both in a week-long school of sport at the old University College Dublin grounds in the centre of that great city.

Many of the great sports champions that I have met and befriended over the years have one denominator in common. They have invariably possessed fertile, highly impressionable imaginations that have been transformed by the chance meeting with a charismatic coach.

For example, the man who in later life would become Commonwealth, European and Olympic long-jump champion (and incidentally, my closest friend), Lynn Davies, as an eighteen- year-old soccer and rugby all-rounder, was spotted by a certain coach called Ron Pickering who told that he could be the best in the world. Likewise another close friend of mine, Lady Mary Peters, Olympic pentathlon champion and world record holder, early in her career fell under the spell of Buster McShane, the most charismatic personality in world sport at the time who came with big ideas and the promise of gold.

Davies and Pickering, Peters and McShane, Herb Elliott and Cerruti, Roger Bannister and Stampfl, Steve Prefontaine and Bowerman, Steve

Ovett and Wilson, Coe and Coe, Jessica Ennis-Hill and Tony Minichiello, the litany of great sports partnerships goes on and on.

For me there was to be no such long-term partnership, mainly because of the nature of my event and the fact that no coach in Ireland or Britain really understood the principles of the newfangled fibre-

With Val McGann with my trophy for winning N. Ireland Decathlon Championship

glass pole which was transforming the event on the other side of the Atlantic. However looking back I was fortunate to encounter several mentors who would have massive psychological impact on my career.

To return to that Dublin school of sport in 1963, there was one of those chance meetings of minds that sparked my over-active imagination and lit the fire of Icarus in my soul. I was there primarily as a 15-year-old, all-round prospect, but I was persuaded to vault in a demonstration for the class by the tall, prematurely greying Irish champion vaulter, Val McGann. Val was a romantic figure, a soft-spoken giant of a man who was also one of the nation's foremost landscape artists …and he could charm the birds out of the trees.

Val had taken delivery of one of the new American fibre-glass 'Skypoles' and enthusiasts from all over the country had come to look at and touch the magic implement as if truly were a sporting talisman. When the demo started the champion encouraged me to try the Skypole, carefully showing me how to hold it in order to achieve the proper bending direction. Not really knowing what I was doing, I responded with a personal best of 10ft 6in, with Val making 12ft. However, it was what the great charmer said that made the difference;

"Michael, you will be Irish Champion one day. You will definitely jump over 14ft."

The important point is that I truly believed him. He had that ability to make you believe, to my mind, still the essence of coaching young people. Give them the dream and make them believe they can achieve it. I left Dublin with a dream and a plan which included getting my hand on one of these new fibreglass poles!

To understand the revolutionary importance of fibreglass poles we need to divert into a short history of the event. You just know I was going to become all nerdy sometime, so the following section is for the purist, or the simply curious!

6. A BRIEF HISTORY OF POLE VAULTING

Pole vaulting first became popular in England in the 1860's, when the very first world record was set by Englishman J. Wheeler with 10ft, using an ash pole with a tripod of iron at the lower end and a technique that enabled him to climb hand over hand and drop over the crossbar.

However the history of the pole vault is primarily one of American domination since the inaugural Olympic Games in Athens in 1896 when William Hoyt took the gold medal with a vault of 10ft 10in and his team-mate, Albert Tyler, the silver with 10ft 8in. Both men used heavy, rigid steel poles. The official report of the event goes;

> After the Greeks had given up the contest (at 9ft 4iin) they became in their turn interested spectators in the contest continued by the two Americans. They were also most energetic in rubbing the limbs of those two champions after each jump. The weather by this time had become so cold that strengthening cordials had to be taken by all the competitors who had taken part in that sport. Massage was also applied to their benumbed limbs.

It is interesting to speculate that the two Americans would probably have been disqualified in the modern arena, as I almost was in the Commonwealth Games, for 'coaching' another competitor; as for 'strengthening cordials', the present paranoia in world athletics would have Olympic Committee members in the throes of seizure at the very thought!

DUTCH

By the 1940s another American, Cornelius 'Dutch' Warmerdam, was setting new standards of vaulting using a more flexible bamboo pole, which had been pioneered by Japanese athletes. Bamboo was lighter and had a bit of a whip, which was advantageous to the agile, fast Dutch, who taped his hand-grip way above that of his peers and broke through the 15ft barrier to establish a truly phenomenal world record height of 15ft 8¾in! (4.79m).

Growing up on a farm in California this child prodigy had been spotted by a track coach driving past the farm. He skidded to halt at what he thought he had just seen. The boy was vaulting into a cabbage patch using a bamboo curtain rod over a make-shift crossbar. The bar was higher than his varsity champion was clearing! That boy was destined to become the best the world had ever seen, and probably ever will see in this event – a much-misused term, but he was certainly a true sporting genius.

Although he never competed in the Olympics, due to a little matter of World War II, Warmerdam was (he died in 2003) indisputably the all-time greatest exponent of leaping with pole. His widow stated that he cleared 16ft in practice, which, if true, is remarkable in view of the fact that the rest of the world was struggling at 14ft and it would be another twenty years before that height was breached in competition. I met him once at the Bakersfield meet in California where this God-like figure, in his role as head coach at Fresno State, was really too preoccupied with the problems of his own college team to have much to say to a lad from Belfast in the bustling changing rooms. For my part, I just shook his hand and stared, no doubt jaw grounded, and thanked the pantheon of gods for granting me an audience with a true sporting deity.

TARZAN

In the decade after Warmerdam, technology got a handle on the event and started the revolution that would change vaulting in a very radical way. Don 'Tarzan' Bragg from the New Jersey outback, USA, was the last metal pole Olympic champion. He won in Rome in 1960 using a lightweight aluminium pole that helped him take the record to over 15ft 9ins (4.81m), beating Warmerdam's record by 2cms; and he did it with some style, making a name for himself by swinging through the trees in the Olympic village yelling the call of the Lord of the Jungle.

With his muscles and shock of black, wavy hair he let it be known that after gold he was heading for Hollywood and that Tarzan role. Now Don really could vault, and he looked the part, but according to legend he failed to convince the producers that he could act. As if acting had anything to do with Tarzan! I am reminded of the Victor Mature story, when, on being refused admission to a posh restaurant which excluded actors, Victor challenged the maitre d' with, "You obviously have not seen any of my movies then?" But in Don's case legend is wrong, as he actually was very good on screen, did all his own stunts of course and completed the movie, '*Tarzan and the Jewel of Opar*', in true professional style, only to be thwarted by legal problems with author Edgar Rice Burroughs's estate. Don passed on to the big jungle in the sky in 2019, age 83, after a life of trials and tribulations, including a sextuple heart bypass, missed and cherished by all, the only Olympic Champion in history to receive his gold medal on the podium with a resounding call of the jungle ape-man.

GLASS FIBRE POLES

In the early Sixties, a relatively unknown Texan called Aubrey Dooley and George Davies from Oklahoma were experimenting with as yet unsanctioned flexible, glass fibre poles. Davies cleared 15ft 10¾in 1961 to eclipse Bragg's mark, prompting Tarzan's retirement amid accusations that this fibreglass stuff was a 'circus act'. The first 16ft vault was achieved in Madison Square Garden indoors in 1962 by John Uelses of the Marines, who, getting what was viewed as the ultimate bend from his implement, surpassed the magic barrier by three quarters of an inch and got a rousing ovation from the standing-room only crowd. Soon after, John Belitza of Southern Illinois University also made 16ft under coach Lew Hartzog, of whom more later.

Outdoors, Uelses repeated his 16-footer but team-mate Dave Tork beat the record with 16ft 2in and the first of the new generation of Europeans, Pentti Nikula of Finland, bettered this with 16ft 2½in. But it was 1963 when more vaulting history was created than any time since Five men went above 16ft indoors in 1963, culminating in Washington State's Brian Sternberg clearing 16ft 3in at Milwaukee. Sternberg's bright star fell, like Icarus in flames, when he was paralyzed in a training accident on a trampoline, sending shockwaves around the world regarding the dangers of the new 'circus act' with its gymnastic training methods. I met Brian later at the Mexico Olympics where, sitting in his wheelchair, he was covering the Games as a journalist and remained philosophical about his fate; there but for the grace of the Gods go all gravity-defiers.

JOHN PENNEL

When the real 1963 outdoor season got under way one man dominated proceedings. John Pennel, a Dade County rope-climbing and sousaphone-playing champion, set global marks of 16ft 3in and 16ft 4in in March and April to start things off. With his strength and gymnastic ability, he had quickly mastered the art of flexible pole jumping. Sternberg came back at him with a 16ft 5in (the world's first 5m vault) in front of 35000 hysterical fans at the Penn Relays, only for Pennel to reply with 16ft 6¾in. The very next week Sternberg went 16ft 8in to end his account on this stage, with Pennel travelling to London's White City Stadium for the GB versus USA match and the prestigious AAA Championships. The rest, as they say, is history with Pennel clearing 16ft 8¾in and 16ft 10¼in in successive competitions, finally returning to Florida to break the 17ft mark by three quarters an inch. The event was on fire!

John Thomas Pennel went on to several more world records, peaking at 17ft 10in in 1969, and an Olympic fifth place in Mexico. His film star features put him in Playboy magazine as the Marlborough Man in the cigarette ads, but he never achieved his ambition of cracking Hollywood. I befriended him during my Churchill Fellowship at the University of California, Los Angeles in 1971 when, although at the end of his athletic career, I found him a wonderfully warm and entertaining companion (he was a talented mimic and would perfectly take off my flat Ulster vowels – a talent, he said, inherited from his Tipperary mother). Pennel ranks alongside Warmerdam and the Ukrainian multi-record breaker, Bubka, as the greatest vaulters of all time. He died prematurely of a cancer and one day I will pay my respects at his graveside.

7. THE IRISH RECORD

Back home in Belfast there was to be no peace for my parents until I had my own fibre-glass pole. The cost, however, was £40, beyond our family's immediate means, so there were many weeks of odd jobs and scrimping and saving until my dad gave mother the money to take me to Clery's Department Store in Dublin to buy my first pole (Why Clery's? I don't know; someone there apparently ordered a batch of fibre poles, possibly on Val McGann's instructions. It was probably the only shop in Europe where you could purchase a fibre-glass vaulting pole.)

The 100-mile trip to Dublin's O'Connell St, the location of Clery's store, was planned by my mother and my Uncle Billy, who had a car, to coincide with a state visit by someone who was second in importance in our family circle only to the Pope himself. John F. Kennedy was the object of mother's adoration and devotion, the Irish American President who, she was sure, would eventually be canonized by the Church. I remember looking out from Clery's shop floor through the big, plate-glass window while handling and flexing my new fibre pole and seeing mother on her brother's shoulders amid the tens of thousands of fellow worshippers lining the pavements of O'Connell St. I saw, but hardly noticed, the youthful, tousle haired J.F.K. and his beautiful wife, Jackie, as their motorcade glided past the window. I had other things on my mind, to do with the 14ft length of glass fibre in my hands. Watch out world, here I come! Little did I know that only a few months later the handsome head glimpsed by me in that limousine would be bloodied and its image splattered across newspapers throughout the world; nor indeed that myself and my flexible friend would be living in the land of hope and glory that had extinguished the young President's life so tragically.

WONDER

I continued to improve as a 16-year-old, with heights of 11ft 3in and 11ft 6in securing Ulster and Irish junior titles and grabbing headlines in the sports pages like; '**WONDER VAULT BY BOY BULL**'

This was penned by the inimitable Ulster sports journalist, Bill Rutherford, who became a friend and one of my biggest supporters. Bill was the one who got me involved with Ulster Television, always pressing the programme makers to give me a shot at commentating and presenting. He secured my long-running column 'Track Talk', with a Sunday newspaper and hounded me relentlessly for copy. It was entirely fitting that Bill shared one of my greatest triumphs, the 1970 Commonwealth Games Gold, when we went together on the mother-of-all celebratory bashes on the town. It was Edinburgh, not Glasgow, that belonged to us that night.

My highest jump that year, 1963, was 11ft 10ins, surprisingly achieved with a borrowed, old metal pole during the World Schools Games in Lisbon. I still managed to win the silver medal but who knows what I might have done had my new fibre pole fitted into the plane at Dublin Airport. This was, however, my introduction to a theme which would fuel a hundred newspaper columns in future years and which was to become a permanent, if unwanted, feature of my life as an international vaulter - the trials and tribulations of having 16ft lengths of tubular fibre-glass as constant travelling companions all over the world.

I suppose it must be something in the psychological make-up of people who succeed in their chosen field, something deep-rooted that compels them to work an idea or an ambition to the utmost, very last degree of effort when more sane mortals would long ago have given up. Today sports psychologists call it 'grit' and they have even invented tests to determine the grit of would-be draft-picks in the American NFL. For example, when I decided to improve my swimming I pestered my father to pick me up at school during the forty minute lunch-break and drive me to the local Falls Road Baths for a strenuous solo twenty minutes of sprint swimming, ten minutes of changing and drying off, and scoffing sandwiches on the five minute drive back to school. I kept this routine up for a year, before athletics became my passion, and not even being caught by the Headmaster, the fearsome, black-frocked figure of Father Walter Larkin, as I charged down the dark corridors, late again from training, wrestling with a scruffy tie-knot, could put me off.

"You are wasting your time with all this sport nonsense, Michael. Concentrate on your books!" Walter would preach to me.

Thankfully, my father and the Headmaster never did see eye to eye on this point, good old dad wholeheartedly embracing the '*mens sana in corpore sano*' philosophy, a sound mind in a sound body.

Dad's credo was certainly put to the test when the younger Bull shifted his attention to athletics. This involved us getting up at 7am for early morning shot and discus sessions at the 'gun pits' behind our estate. This was the site of the wartime anti-aircraft bunkers, a great natural playground for the kids of the district and a great training ground for a budding athlete as there were acres of concrete on which to throw my implements. As dad was an AAA senior coach in the throws I quickly progressed, setting Irish junior records of 57ft 6in for the 10lb shot and 163ft for the 1kg discus.

In pole-vaulting, however, I was still very much a solo act with my 14ft. long, 150lb-test fibre pole. The test weight of a pole is the calibration used to identify what body weight a vaulter should be to safely bend the pole. As I already weighed 12 stone (168lb) there was no way my pole was not going to bend through 90 degrees once I got on it. Knowing this, the Northern Ireland athletics association selected me to go to the annual Young Athletes Course at Lilleshall during the Easter holiday in 1964. This produced the greatest formative experience of my sporting life. I met Ron and Lynn.

LILLESHALL

The cream of Britain's young athletics talent attended the course in the beautiful grounds of an old English country mansion, converted to provide training facilities for a variety of sports. I was the only boy doing the highly unusual mix of shot, discus and vault, a fact that no coach seemed to pick up on – I never heard the word 'decathlon' mentioned. Most of my time and energy was spent in the throwing circles, being alternately overwhelmed by the older and much bigger English 'heavies'

Trevor Burton, first Briton over 15ft

and terrified by the gigantic (he was almost 7ft tall) international shot-putter and coach, John Savage. Then one day I was approached by the National Coach in charge of the course, Ron Pickering, who said he had heard that I could bend these new fibre-glass poles and he would like me to demonstrate, along with British senior champion, Trevor Burton, in front of the entire ensemble of Britain's finest young athletes.

I was very nervous. Trevor demonstrated his sort of hybrid, straight metal pole technique mixed with a rather tentative fibre-glass bend, easily clearing 14ft. I was next up. It was quite a surprise to Trevor, Ron and everyone else when this boy stepped forward holding Trevor's 15ft pole right at the top end, and, with no measured run-up or recognizable technique, proceeded to charge fearlessly at the box (the 8in deep trough into which the pole is planted on take-off). As the implement bent through 90 degrees and flipped its carrier spectacularly into the air, there was a gasp from the audience. Trevor was sure his best pole was about to snap, Ron that one of his charges was about to die, and the rest simply had never seen anything like this before.

Not having the faintest idea of what to do next or how to control flight, I crashed into the crossbar and landed with an unceremonious thump in the pit, amazingly still in one piece. Ron rushed to my side, his majestic voice booming with a mixture of pride and enthusiasm,

"You know you almost cleared 13ft"

My personal best at the time was 11ft 10in. As I bathed in the glory of my new-found status, I prayed to the gods that I would not be asked for a repeat performance. The uncoiled power in that inert piece of glass fibre had frightened the wits out of me ...but I sort of liked the danger and I knew that I would do it again, only with more control.

This was Ron Pickering's gift, a bit of bluff and bluster combined with an indefatigable enthusiasm. He had a rare ability to con athletes into doing the near impossible, admitting that the East End wide-boy was only just beneath the surface of the urbane teacher. He understood the highly impressionable nature of the minds of young athletes and used established internationals to work with us and to demonstrate their techniques in person. He had invited one such star to the course to do a long-jump demo. Thus began the first day of the rest of my life.

LYNN

When Lynn Davies was introduced by Ron to us as we sat in a neat line along the runway, he immediately appeared to me to be the perfect embodiment of the concept 'athlete'. A lithe but immensely powerful and muscular six- footer with striking good looks, the Welsh and British champion ran like a cheetah and gave such an immediate impression of awesome explosive energy and power. Even when he scrambled out of the sand pit and walked back to check his run-up markers, this creature moved with a cat-like poise and balance. This was a species I had never seen before. All those other champions I had been reading about, like Don 'Tarzan' Bragg, Dutch Warmerdam, Al Oerter and Dallas Long, Olympic discus and shot champions respectively, must be like this too.

I watched the cat's every movement during that demo, the way he straightened his white socks (much whiter than my dirty school gym socks), the slapping of his tanned thighs (as opposed to my mottled ones) as he stood at the end of the runway to engender the psyche-up, the high knees sprinting action (this must be the key to running that fast), and the carefree wave to the spellbound audience on completion of yet another gravity-defying leap. There was also that distinctive red and blue hooped white athletics vest, which announced that here was a Great Britain International Athlete (it actually said on the vest *Great Britain And Northern Ireland*.)

I resolved there and then that nothing mattered more than getting one of those vests myself and, more than that, wearing it just like the

long-jumper performing for us. I wanted to look just like him and to be just like him.

What I did not know, of course, was the months of torturous weight-lifting, sand-hill running, circuit training, gymnastics, interval speed-endurance work, sprinting and technique work that Lynn, with his coach driving him on (Ron of course), had endured in order to look

Olympic Gold Medalist Lynn Davies in his prime at the White City in 1965.

like that. They were working with only one objective in mind, the Olympic Games to be held later that year, 1964, in Tokyo.

I was soon to find out, along with the rest of the sports world, just how much sheer hard work and single-minded determination, most of it in the climatically unfavourable environs of South Wales on rain-sodden runways and wind-swept tracks, it had taken for the Welshman to become an Olympic Champion.

Some six months after that Lilleshall demonstration, Lynn was to cut through rain and headwind on a drenched cinder runway in the Japanese capital and beat the world's best jumpers in the Olympic final.

Lynn Davies became a sporting immortal as he figuratively ascended Mount Olympus to don the laurel wreath of Olympic Champion. I too wanted to be one.

Val McGann continued to encourage me throughout those early times, predicting that I would surpass 15ft and 16ft when to me those celestial heights seemed impossible. He was present at the College Races in Dublin in 1966 when, at age 19, I became the first Irishman to clear 15ft finishing second to the new UK National record of 15ft 3in set by my friend and early international partner, David Stevenson. We received our prizes and congratulations from the revered Irish President, Eamonn de Valera, and, along with Val, celebrated long into the night.

It is worthy of note that these heights were achieved jumping from a grass run-up and landing in a sand and scrap rubber pit. Val gave me one of his early landscapes of the Antrim Coast in recognition of my performance. He subsequently emigrated to the USA, opened an art gallery with his wife in New England and became an acclaimed artist. Val passed on in 2016 and we had a lovely farewell phone conversion with much talk of both of us making an athletic comeback; gone but not forgotten.

8. ILLINOIS ODYSSEY

Young people growing up in the sixties were swamped by American popular culture, from the new beat music of the likes of Elvis Presley, Fats Domino, Ricky Nelson, Fabian, Eddie Cochrane, to be heard on crackling wireless sets on stations like Radio Luxembourg, to the shining new stars of the silver screen. Brando and Dean were the heavyweights but there were also the teen idols like Tab Hunter, Troy Donahue, Ty Hardin, Will Hutchins and Clint Walker, who could be seen on the flickering black and white television tubes that were becoming popular. My half sister, Kathleen, who emigrated at the age of 20 to New York to become an Irish nanny, the ultimate status symbol for a successful American family, kept me posted on the vicissitudes of the great American way of life. I was totally aware of the possibility that sport could make dreams of America come true. Ronnie Delaney had left Dublin in the early 1950s with an athletic scholarship to the USA's Villanova University and returned home with an Olympic gold medal for the 1500m from the 1956 Melbourne Games.

At 17 I had completed my A Levels and was busy that summer, 1964, winning the Irish pole-vault title, with a record 12ft 11in at Dublin's Santry Stadium and becoming the first Irishman to clear 13ft (4m) at Belfast's Aircraft Park. The super-sequence press photo of the latter clearly shows the small pile of sand surrounded by concrete paving stones standing on end, which constituted the landing area. Talk about reckless endangerment! There were also a couple of glimpses of the future during that summer of '64. I became the youngest ever decathlon champion of Northern Ireland, on my first attempt at the gruelling two-day contest, and that pole went missing again somewhere between Dublin and

Gerona, in Spain, venue of the World Schools Games. I recall a trip to some distant Spanish customs holding centre in the Volkswagen Beetle belonging to Pete Davidson and Bill Baillie, two school athlete friends who were in Gerona on holiday, and the triumphant retrieval of the precious pole, just in time for my vault final. I thanked the boys the best way possible with a new Irish record of 13ft 1in and first place. They were to see repeat performances of this later when I was to join them as a fellow member of The Queen's University of Belfast Athletics Club.

It was around this time that I had gained my first Irish international vests against Belgium and Scotland, in Brussels, and against England at Crystal Palace. Each was to provide formative experience.

The Belgian meet introduced me to the charismatic British record holding Scot, David Stevenson, who, out on the town for a few post-match bevies with some of his team, was surprised to run into a naive but enthusiastic young Bull all alone at a Brussels night club. Arms around

Pole Vaulters in Belfast for a meeting at Paisley Park L-R Myself, Trevor Burton, Trevor's fiancée Judy Cornwell and British record holder David Stevenson

two glamorous club hostesses, I was sipping a glass of fine champagne and beckoning Dave to join me. He did so and laughingly inquired as to who was paying for the drinks; "I don't know. Probably the girls," I suggested, to which Dave replied, somewhat more sternly, "Right, Seamus (his new name for me) when I say 'go', just jump up and run like hell for the door!" We did so in a flurry of unbridled athleticism, escaping into the night, a friendship forged forever. This boy was obviously going places… but where?

David Stevenson remains in contact with me from his Laird's manor in the Borders. The second Briton, after England's Trevor Burton, to vault 15ft, David got a degree in accountancy from Edinburgh University and created from scratch a dynasty, the Edinburgh Woolen Mill conglomerate. I have been privileged on the odd occasion to dine at the Laird's table and to tell sporting tales to bring a flush to the Master's face; but then again, his sainted wife, Alix (nee Jamison), herself an Olympic long-jumper, has heard it all before.

The other international, at London's Crystal Palace, taught an altogether different lesson. I had taken delivery of a new, stronger pole, courtesy of Courage breweries, and was expected to do well, but all evening I had terrible difficulties with my run-up. Measured to the inch, a jumper's run-up ensures that his take-off foot lands in right place and being either too close in or too far away at take-off is potentially disastrous in an event that can punish technical errors not only with a poor performance but with physical injury. A compatriot suggested I re-measure to the training shoe that marked my run-up distance, for he had noticed an older and somewhat embittered ex-record holder moving my shoe out of place. I did so but remained unsettled throughout the competition, not achieving the heights that would have been within reach. Gamesmanship it was called. I did not like it and never resorted to it in that way throughout my record-setting 69 internationals for Great Britain.

ATHLETIC SCHOLARSHIP

Later that summer, when I had taken my record to 13ft 4in, the mercurial little Dubliner, Billy Morton, who really put Santry Stadium on the world map with Australian miler Herb Elliott's record-breaking races there against all-comers, invited me to compete against a touring US team. They were in Europe to catch some warm-up competition prior to the Tokyo Olympic Games, and among their champions was world vault record holder, at 17ft 2in, Texan Fred Hansen. I did not see Fred at all as I worked up to 13ft 1in (failing narrowly at an Irish mark of 13ft 5in) because he did not take his start until 15ft! He then attempted the astronomical 16ft and made it on his fourth and unofficial attempt, preferring to stop there and not risk injury in the small Santry landing area made up with sand and rubber scraps.

I was mesmerized, and somewhat shy, but I steeled myself to wish the 'great one' luck. The Rice University dentistry graduate looked me in the eyes, thanked me and drawled, "You must run hard at the box, use your abdominal muscles to rock back on the pole and look up at that ole blue sky." As he spoke, he pulled up his US vest and flashed a six-pack that made a washboard look smooth. I wanted abdominals just like those!

If the great Fred Hansen had not much noticed the 17 year- old kid jumping over 13ft at Santry that night, someone else certainly did. Lew Hartzog, the coach in charge of this USA team on its mission to the Tokyo Olympics, approached me and congratulated me on a fine performance. A proud Texan like Fred, the words which drawled from that craggy, sunburnt face remain clear, "How'd y'all like to come and study at Illinois with me?" At first I was not sure if Lew meant myself and all the other athletes milling around, but no, the Southern "y'all" clearly referred to yours truly, alone. I gulped and I think the words "Yes, please" did eventually come out! My father was consulted at trackside and he told Lew that it all depended on the results of my A' Levels. Pass and he can go; fail and he repeats the year at St Malachy's. I think I quickly found religion again because many prayers and only a few weeks later my desired results came through and the contracts for my joining Southern Illinois University were signed. Full fees and tuition, room and board and training and competition were all in the deal, 'the full ride' in America-speak. All I had to do was to vault well and maintain an academic 'C' average. I was on my way to the USA.

IN JAMES DEAN'S BACKYARD

The Southern Illinois University was a large state college of some 25,000 students, based in the small southern town of Carbondale. The flight was by jet to New York and onwards in a smaller plane to St Louis, Missouri, where I was met by one of the university's senior track stars, the English sub-four-minute miler, Bill Cornell, who was to drive me to Carbondale. At the arrivals hall, Bill was holding up a large card with the name 'Mick O'Bull' writ large. I approached but never corrected my name. I was still 17 years young. This was like being on another planet, the extensive campus set along the banks of man-made lakes, the halls of residence, the fraternity and sorority houses, the futuristic sports dome and football stadium, surrounded by an eight-lane athletics track. I was very impressed with the large, foam rubber pole-

1964, aged 17 at the Southern Illinois University pole vault pit which allowed you to focus on leaping the maximum height as opposed to the British pits of the time where the vaulters fucus tended to be more on surviving the landing!

vault pit and the fast, bitumen runways that I had only read about in magazines. It was warm and sunny. It was the sort of place that I imagined all those incredible American performances, the ones you would read about in 'Athletics Weekly' magazine, could actually happen. It was the sort of place where trackmen with the splendidly onomatopoeic names like Bob Sprung (vaulter), Larry Hendershott (shot-putter), and Bud Held (javelin thrower) would achieve incredible vaults and throws.

The great thing about the scholarship, as I was about to find out, after standing in line for hours along with thousands of other freshmen registering for lecture courses, was that athletes do not have lectures between two and five o'clock each day; that's when they train. The downside was that you had to do a job on the athletes' work programme, like cleaning the kit room at 7.30 in the morning or selling programmes at the intervarsity basketball games, or measuring 'downs' on the football field during the packed gridiron games. I soon learned the pecking order in American sport, footballers the real stars, basketball players just behind (although one of our freshmen was the future pro star Walt Frazier) and way down on the list were the track and field jocks.

WORK, TRAIN AND PLAY

The head coach decided that I would be better living in a fraternity house rather than conventional halls of residence, which could be impersonal and lonely places. So, I entered the 'Sigma Pi' house, an idyllically appointed domicile on the shore of a boating and fishing lake, home to some 40-odd lost souls. They were all crazy, as I was to discover during 'hell-week', when the initiates were subjected to the most brutal and horrific ritual degradation at the hands of the senior brothers. They were deprived of sleep, soap and water, proper food and had to wear sackcloth while in the house, itching and scratching at their vomit and urine-stained skin. In the dead hours of one night the dormitory, where all 40 of us slept on bunk beds, was shaken by a series of loud explosions. The post-Cuban Crisis early 60s was a period of precarious world nuclear threats and I was sure the Russians had launched a pre-emptive strike. I leapt from my bed and crawled under the bunks, cowering from the inferno. Then the lights went on and the brothers all burst into the dorm and rounded up all the terrified 'pledges', the initiates, taking them down into the basement for more unspeakable mutual urine-drinking and vomiting down each other's sackcloth shirts. The last of the firecrackers popped harmlessly in the dorm and the rest of us went back to sleep. Quite good preparation really for future life in various Games villages!

It is worth saying that the general impression within British sport at the time was that US scholarships presented some sort of utopia for the budding athlete, where the very best facilities and equipment were matched by expert specialist coaching and technical analysis. The university system there was viewed, along with the state-sponsored sport culture of the old Soviet Union and Eastern Bloc, as being fully 'professional' in the derogatory sense that made it somehow cheating when compared with our amateurs. Certainly, in America the time to train was set firm and an athletic scholarship guaranteed you an education if you produced the sporting goods. However, coaching in technical events was generally way behind Britain at that time and facilities were not always ideal. At Illinois, for example, where winters were extremely cold, there were no indoor training facilities and the only coaching we jumpers and throwers got was from our team-mates.

The real difference lay in the fiercely competitive intervarsity sports programme. Regular indoor and outdoor competitions all over the Mid-West area, referred to as the 'conference', took the team to university towns from Chicago to Austin, Texas, with stops in between in Kansas, Oklahoma, Indiana, Missouri, Kentucky and Tennessee. And in almost every one of these track and field venues there was a freshman vaulter who could jump higher than me. The press clippings from home proclaiming *'Wonder vault by boy Bull'* were soon forgotten in the very sobering experience of learning one's trade in the competitive cauldron of collegiate athletics. The kind of workman-like toughness that this American experience engendered was to become my trademark throughout what was to become the longest of international careers.

There was fun as well. Southern Illinois University tried very hard to live up to its fifth-place national ranking in the Playboy list of top party colleges. There was the very American undergraduate practice of the 'panty raid', where the lads of a fraternity would storm a neighbouring, female sorority house and, rifling through the drawers and cupboards amid the shrieking protests of the girls, collect as many trophy pairs of knickers as could be carried. There was also the reciprocal collective 'moon shot,' not an experiment in astrophysics, as you may have thought, rather an invitation to a sorority garden party at precisely 10.00pm, where the expectant males would turn up to a totally dark and deserted garden. At the appointed time the darkness would be split open by the carefully synchronized switching on of all lights at the top floor bedroom windows, against which the pristine and very naked derrières of the sisterhood would be collectively pressed. The lad from St Malachy's was shocked and delighted in equal measure.

Other aspects of American life and culture were more disturbing. An illegal beer party by a lake (illegal because under Illinois liquor laws you had to be over 21 to purchase or consume alcohol) came to an abrupt end for me when the girl with whom I was fumbling on the grass screamed in my ear – not due to my actions, but rather, as a result of being prodded by a man carrying a torch and a large hessian sack; "What y'all doin' down there?" he enquired, shining the light in our startled eyes. "I wouldn't be there if I were you," he volunteered, as he opened the sack a little to show us the dozen or so deadly cottonmouth snakes he had been busily collecting along the shores of the lake. In two shakes of a cottonmouth's tail I was out of there, terrified and rather ungallantly abandoning my companion in our moment of passion. You see, there are no snakes in Ireland, thanks to good old St Patrick, or so my mother fervently believed.

That first year at Illinois produced the desired effect with the 14ft barrier being breached by some three inches for a new Irish mark and a third- place ranking among British seniors. More congenial living quarters, shared with newly arrived English triple jumper, John Vernon, seemed also to help the academic side of things, with my end of year studies resulting in the Dean's High Academic Achievement award. John Vernon was to become a collegiate star in his very European event and eventually married the Illinois athlete to whom I had supplied the initial introduction, the later Commonwealth champion hurdler, Judy Vernon. As for myself, an unlucky injury to British number one, Dave Stevenson, put me next in line for international consideration. Suddenly that blue, red and white hooped vest that I had for so long coveted was within reach.

9. THE FIRST OF SIXTY-NINE

Northern Ireland is a very strange place.

Its people are universally recognized as the kindest and most hospitable on earth. This, of course, has not prevented them from maiming and killing each other, in the name of one God or another for years.

It has a population of about 1.75 million but seems to have produced a disproportionately large number of successful people in the fields of literature and the arts, academia and entertainment and, of course, in sport.

Without too much effort one could come up with literary figures from CS Lewis to Bernard McLaverty to Seamus Heaney, film stars from Errol Flynn to Liam Neeson, musicians from, James Galway to Van Morrison and so the list could go on.

In the world of sport, the list is endless with stars in soccer, rugby, motorsport, golf, boxing and many other sports including of course my own athletics.

One might well ask why. What set of environmental and cultural factors conspire to produce so many talented performers emanating from such a geographically remote and demographically impoverished little province? Some rather uncharitable commentators have suggested that it is this very starkness that has forced talent to the fore, to escape the dire circumstances, certainly of the last 35 odd years, if nothing else.

There may some truth in the notion of social hardship providing a great motivating impetus for individuals to succeed in their chosen dimension, certainly we have little else going for us. In terms of Darwinian natural selection, success in sport is possible only to the few with the requisite physical and psychological qualities. These qualities are highly specialized and specific to the types of sporting activities. I mean to say, Harlem has never produced a black Alex Higgins and Belfast has never produced a white Tommy Smith. There are cultural and physiological factors determining all this, but the weight of evidence suggests that in sport genetics and physiology rule supreme. Belfast may never produce a world-record sprinter or vaulter but there could well be a future world snooker champion from a black ghetto.

THE PETERS ENIGMA

Let me put it in another way. If you were to produce an ideal blueprint for a young, talented athlete to become the greatest all-round athlete in the world, to become a world-record holder and Olympic champion in say the pentathlon (the five-event multi-discipline before the present seven-event heptathlon), first of all, you would not choose one Mary Elizabeth Peters; not simply because she was living, going to school and on to college in the athletics backwater that was Northern Ireland in the fifties; not nearly tall enough, not as tall as Heidi Rosendahl or Burglinde Polak, the two German Aryans who finished behind her in Munich. Not well-enough endowed with natural co-ordination or all-round sporting ability, not as physically blessed as England's Mary Rand, who won a silver medal in Tokyo's pentathlon and set a world record in the long-jump, Mary Peters hated changes in technique enforced by her coach, Buster McShane. She was told by a famous national coach at a young athletes' course to "stick to hockey", as she would never make it as an athlete. That coach, the legendary Geoff Dyson, was made to remember those words by the victor at one of the many celebratory functions following her ultimate triumph where I was a guest. He was suitably embarrassed, of course, but quickly recovered composure to claim that he was merely applying 'negative reinforcement' to motivate the young Mary. Risky strategy I'd say!

Mary's training facility in a Portadown field included a concrete shot circle laid by her father at the back of her home rather than the magnificent National Stadia of her international rivals. And then there

A far cry from Munich – a young Mary Peters training in the field behind her house

was the savagery and brutality of the bombs and bullets of Belfast in the sixties and seventies, during the most crucial years of her sporting life. Not the privileged training camps of the Masters of Sport in the Soviet Bloc, or even the leafy suburbs of Crystal Palace, but rather the armed barricades outside the gym in Belfast and her Antrim Road flat where I would leave her home after training every night. Her accommodation was in the same building as a flat to which three young British soldiers were lured to their deaths on March 9th 1971 by the feminine charms of their slayers and the promise of something more alluring than a bullet in the back of the head. The eternal hall light that shone for years in the flat next to hers was a ghostly testament to the terrorist 'honeypot'.

For Mary there were no great indoor sports halls like Stuttgart, the Los Angeles Forum, the French Sports Institute at Vincennes or even the athletics paradise that now resides at the University of Wales in Cardiff, or indeed the fantastic facilities in many UK cities from London to Sheffield. The Shore road hockey pitches, often a rain-sodden or snow-bound mess of cinders and dirt, was our training venue for much of the winter. As for expert coaching, a coach was someone who would dig the shot out of the muddy hole in the ground and produce a rag with which to clean it for the next effort, not the highly paid technical analyst who would film and examine your skills each session, as in East Germany then and in Britain now. In any case, the typical international coach was unlikely to be a self-educated ex-shipyard worker with no background in the sport itself and no official accreditation of any sort at all in the grand corridors of influence.

So, on this blueprint there would seem to be no hope of success at all; no facilities or equipment, inadequate sporting infrastructure, no specialized planning or technical coaching, no 'proper' coach and no genetically superior physical specimen on which to work. Completely hopeless, and completely typical of the perversity of the human condition; Beethoven, the greatest composer of music was deaf; Michelangelo, the greatest painter, almost blind at the end; the greatest comedian, Tony Hancock, a tortured depressive. The Olympic hammer throwing champion, Hal Connolly from the USA, had a withered arm. The ones who do it, who succeed, use adversity to their advantage, so why should the greatest all-round female athlete in the world not come from Belfast? Who knows, perhaps Dyson's comment sparked the burning need for revenge in an impressionable young psyche. Perhaps Buster, the former shipyard welder who raged in a similarly vengeful way against his social and educational disadvantages, provided the spark.

After winning the Decathlon in Christchurch, New Zealand, I was interviewed on New Zealand television by a local presenter: "How do you explain the fact that Northern Ireland, one of the smallest countries in the Commonwealth, has produced the greatest all-round female athlete (Mary had previously won the Pentathlon) and now the greatest all-round male athlete in the Games? It's like the Faroe Islands winning the World Cup!"

DESIRE

Of course, the question was unanswerable, at least in a convenient journalistic sort of way. We were not products of an acknowledged athletics tradition, nor pupils of a world-renowned national sports institute, we didn't have a coaching guru (coach Buster McShane had died a year before). No, the reasons for our success were more rooted in personal desire and determination and a genuine love for the events we were doing, what has been called 'grit', defined as 'passion and perseverance for a long term goal' (see Amit Katwala's *The Athletic Brain* for more on this).

Certainly, for me the pole vault was the one great enduring love affair of my life. That natural aptitude of the risk-seeker who could fly through the air on the end of a pole that emerged on the school football pitch, gradually progressed to the serious study of the minutiae of the event; from the American dominated history of the great exponents to the notoriously complex double pendulum mechanics of vaulting (the swinging pole being one pendulum, the attached swinging body of the vaulter being the other). It was always the most spectacular event in the arena – often held close to the crowd on one side of the track, with the muscular sprinting gymnasts who performed it often looking like extroverted exhibitionists playing to that crowd. They were sort of removed from the rest of the events, like a private club with special rules and paraphernalia. They were the trapeze artists of this circus – and how the crowd loved them.

Despite my natural introversion, I wanted to belong to that exclusive club. In early training sessions, alone with an aluminium pole and a piece of rope draped for a crossbar set out at about nine feet high, I would pretend to be Bob Richards, the American dubbed the Vaulting Vicar, who, I had read, stood at the end of the runway praying and asking God not to let his trailing finger brush the bar off again. Well, it seemed to work for him, the double Olympic champion of 1952 and 1956.

The sort of desire involved here, of a young lad deeply wanting to be good at his sport, to be acclaimed, famous and successful, is nothing new in a land of soccer hopefuls. A young lad exactly the same age as me, in a different school, in another part of the same city, had similar fantasies with a tennis ball for a football; George Best had dreams too. I was lucky enough to be one of a small number to have their sporting dreams come true although, given the bafflingly esoteric nature of my chosen sport, I was probably the only teenager in the country with these particular dreams.

Part of that dream was winning a United Kingdom vest, not for any nationalistic sentiments, but simply that it was a badge of honour and status, a measure of progress that one was at least second best exponent of the event in the country (most international matches were two-a-side). It was a passport to more foreign competitions, the only way to learn and improve the mysterious technique of this event. It was the necessary first step on the road to becoming one of the best vaulters in the world. However, it was how you took this first step that mattered. Many athletes, especially in this unpredictable activity, failed at the first hurdle or, worse, became what is known in popular culture as 'one-hit wonders'.

POLEAXED FOR POLAND

By mid-summer of 1965 I was, at 18, still a junior, firmly in line for selection to the Great Britain team. Trevor Burton, the first Briton to clear 15ft, was clearly number one. But with UK record-holder Stevenson sidelined through injury, the second spot on the team looked like being mine. My 14ft ¼in Irish record at Paisley Park in Belfast, on returning from Illinois, was the second highest by a Briton. However, in my first British AAA championships at the famous White City, I was mesmerized by watching the amazing American vaulter, Paul Wilson (who had jumped 16ft at high school!), and was beaten for the minor placings by the Army's Jeff Fenge and Loughborough's Martin Higdon, 14ft to 13ft 6in.

The selectors went strictly on form and picked Fenge to partner Burton in the first match of the season against Poland at the White City. I was suicidal. Jeff was in and I was out, and I figured that I would have to jump a lot higher to break though, to give those faceless selectors no room for doubt in the future. I continued to train hard and then the break came, though not in a way that any vaulter would wish on another. It is in the nature of the event that it is a bit hit and miss; wind, rain, run- up soft spots and fear, yes fear, is a real factor in the only event that repays technical errors with injury. I mean, you literally can break your neck if you miss the pit. Anyway, for whatever reason, nerves and all the rest, Jeff failed to clear his opening height against Poland and thus scored nil points for Great Britain. Jeff was a lovely lad and a talented athlete, a fellow gravity-defier against whom I would compete for many subsequent years, but that first international vest was also his last.

HUNGRY FOR HUNGARY

The next international match in this 1965 season was Great Britain v. Hungary, scheduled for 13th and 14th August at London's White City. The letter dropped into the hallway of my home at 23 Sunninghill Drive

BRITISH AMATEUR ATHLETIC BOARD

(Affiliated to the I.A.A.F. as the Governing Athletic Association for the United Kingdom of Great Britain and Northern Ireland)

Constituent Members:
AMATEUR ATHLETIC ASSOCIATION
SCOTTISH AMATEUR ATHLETIC ASSOCIATION
NORTHERN IRELAND AMATEUR ATHLETIC ASSOCIATION

President: H.R.H. THE PRINCE PHILIP, DUKE OF EDINBURGH, K.G., K.T., G.B.E.

Chairman
J. W. TURNER

Honorary Treasurer:
H. M. ABRAHAMS, C.B.E.

Honorary Secretary,
A. A. GOLD

Honorary Team Manager:
L. R. W. GOLDING

Clerk to the Board
Miss M. TUFFHOLME

Telephone: LANgham 3493
Telegrams: ATHLETE, LONDON, W.1

26, PARK CRESCENT,
LONDON,
W.1.

2nd August, 1965.

Dear Michael

I have pleasure in informing you that you have been selected to represent Great Britain and Northern Ireland in the match with Hungary to take place at the White City Stadium on Friday evening and Saturday afternoon, August 13th and 14th in the following event(s):

Pole Vault
....

on.... Saturday ....

I congratulate you upon your selection and shall be glad to learn by the speedy return of the form attached that this is an invitation which you are able to accept.

Yours sincerely,

Arthur Gold.

The first of seventy,

on the third of August. It was the first of 69 such letters (70 actually, as one against Finland in 1972 was discounted due to my getting injured during the warm-up) which were to constitute an unbroken run of GB vests, a record of 69 international appearances for my country.

And what had made the difference? Well, that first chance, on that first international, produced a very rare one-two placing for Britain in

The first of 69 international vests age 18 versus Hungary in in 1965. I finished 2nd with a vault of 4.30m . Note the notorious White City landing pit in the background with its concrete surround.

the pole vault against supposedly superior European jumpers. Burton won with 14ft 9in and I was second with a new Irish and British junior record of 14ft 1in. I had risen to the occasion. I had taken my chance. I had felt very much at home in this famous stadium and, in the vault pit in which I knew the legendary John Pennel of the USA had set two world records of 16ft 8in and 16ft 10in back in 1963. I had liked the cut of that hooped vest on my shoulders and the exclusivity of the small Union Flag on the corner of my new blue cotton British track suit, the free Adidas shoes and spikes given to us for the occasion, the free air tickets from Belfast to London Heathrow. I also liked my new team-mates, many of whom were household names, like Lynn Davies and Mary Rand, sprinters David and Ron Jones, miler Alan Simpson, 400 metre hurdler and Olympic silver medallist John Cooper, another Olympic silver man, steeple-chaser Maurice Herriott, distance men Ron Hill and Bruce Tulloh, sprinter Dorothy Arden and ladies' captain Mary Peters, and the glamorous Janet Simpson in the 400 metres.

THE INITIATION

The initiation on the track had gone well. My evening initiation at the traditional post-match dinner had more mixed reviews. The first point to make is that the British athletics team then was much more of a team than it is today. International matches against the likes of Poland and Germany, the USSR and the USA, together with the major Games of Olympic, European and Commonwealth Championships, were the only big meetings. There were no Grand Prix or Diamond League events and precious few international meets, so this group of 50 or so men and women travelled, ate, slept and lived together for much of the year – well, metaphorically at least, because in truth it was not cool to be seen sitting beside one of the ladies on a plane, much less showing amorous inclinations towards one. That was before the meet ('meet' is American shorthand for 'meeting', meaning 'competition'). After competition and the ritual post-meet drinks, well, anything was possible!

By the time we got to the Dorchester Hotel for the team reception and dinner, we were already flying fairly high. It had been a typically hot and humid August day in London and the first pint in the wee bar at our hotel, the Windsor at Lancaster Gate, had not touched flesh on its speedy decent to the innermost caverns of my gullet. A couple more in the bath and my teammate, Trevor, reared on best ale at Stoke-on-Trent, and myself, a virtual teetotaller, were already 'happy'. We were all fairly dehydrated after the day's activity, especially in view of the fact that I never remember anyone drinking water! Strange as it may seem today, when people cannot get to the car to go shopping without sucking on the nipple of an isotonically- prepared water bottle, athletes then did not drink water before or during competition and training! Afterwards, well, anything was possible – even water.

Dehydrated or not, the first bottle of red wine at the reception went down fairly swiftly, unhindered as it was by any food on the way down, certainly not by the raw fish that had quickly been returned to the plate from whence it had come; smoked salmon, I was told, a rare delicacy. There had been no lunch, pre-competition nerves rendering all thoughts of food repulsive. By this time, the dark, Romany looks of the amazon on the table opposite us were beginning to beguile. Nor had my Irish bonhomie and youthful exuberance gone unnoticed by the old salts of the team. 'Coop' (John Cooper) kept my glass full and my attention focussed with tales of this Slavic wench's sexual prowess and the whisper circulating that she had eyes for me. Burton and Davies, and Mary P. may have had a hand in it also, confirmed that I was on to a sure thing and had to make my move after the last, riveting speech by team chief, Arthur Gold.

It was not so much that my nerve was fortified by all the revelry, more a case of my innate sensibilities being anaesthetized, that I was able to broach the immortal, first chat-up line, "Like a drink?"

The response was positive, that is if you count the sudden appearance of several more bottles of red, allied to the fact that most of it was disposed of in short shrift by my thirsty companion. Things were looking up but I should have paid more attention at St Malachy's to Shakespeare who remarked on alcohol, "it provokes the desire, but it takes away the performance". Oh the follies of youth!

PROGRESS

There were to be many more international appearances for Britain and NI all throughout the 1966 and 1967 seasons. I have already dealt with the former in chapter 1, detailing that decisive first Commonwealth Games medal in Jamaica. Later in that year I also made my first European Championships Final in Budapest. The 1967 season was a hectic pre-Olympic whirlwind with a visit to Los Angeles to represent the Commonwealth against the mighty USA, and a long flight to Tokyo for the World Student Games. It was here that I broke the UK record again with 15ft 9ins (4.80m), the same height as American world record holder Bob Seagren, of whom more later. However, along with this success came more practical problems concerning these greater heights and poor facilities at home for training and competing. Let's examine this next.

10. PHILOSOPHY AND SPORT

Imagine standing on top of a London double-decker bus, 15ft 1in (4.60m) above the ground, and then falling off backwards on to a small pile of sand bordered by concrete paving stones neatly fixed upright on edge to create a nice, sharp container for the sand, almost like a pillow to catch the brain matter that would inevitably be spilled.

This became my stock reply to questions from the athletics press about lagging British vault standards. This suicide mission was being asked

While better than a sandpit surrounded by concrete, the landing at Crystal Palace c. 1968 was still somewhat of a lottery.

of me, week in week out, throughout the sixties as I increased the British record from Dave Stevenson's 15ft 3ins (4.65m) to 15ft 6ins(4.75m), and on to 15ft 9in (4.80m) and through the 16ft (4.90m), 16ft 6in (5m) and 17ft barriers (5.20m).

THE CAMPAIGN

In the UK, a nation where the athletics tradition was firmly rooted in a harrier mentality, running was foremost, and running, whether for long or short distances, over obstacles or country terrain, does not require specialist facilities. It certainly did not require compressed rubber landing areas, crossbars and stands on which to place them at some 17ft in height, and all the annoying little technicalities that this new breed of pole vaulting circus performers were demanding. As one of the leading exponents of the sport I too was demanding these things and for a while was undeservedly gaining the reputation for being difficult and 'big-headed', but it was my head and my neck that were at risk.

So began a sort of one-man campaign to change the thinking and to try to improve vault facilities throughout the country, in an effort to make the White City or Crystal Palace jumping areas more like their American or European equivalents. Two incidents will serve to illustrate the problems of the day, which, to a modern athlete, must read like something from Homer's *Iliad*, the epic poem set during the Trojan War about the quarrel between King Agamemnon and the warrior Achilles. I aspired to the Achilles role.

The first incident happened in May 1968, right in the middle of finals at Queen's University Belfast, the historic seat of learning to which I had transferred from Southern Illinois two years earlier. By this time I was British champion and record-holder (by quite a margin) and had recently cleared 16ft 1¾in to become the first Briton to clear the sixteen foot barrier indoors, at the draughty old converted hangar at R.A.F. Cosford, which was the only indoor competition arena in the country.

The whole sporting world, including myself, was eagerly anticipating the Olympic Games, scheduled for that summer in the atmospherically challenged Mexico City. My own sense of anticipation was heightened by the arrival of an invitation from the British Board to a competition in Nairobi, Kenya, which was an inopportunely-timed invitation, right in the middle of exams. However, this was one invitation which was really worthy of careful consideration as Nairobi, like Mexico, was at altitude.

It really is a measure of the innocence of the times that we simply knew very little about the effects of altitude on physical performance, especially in the area of the shorter, more explosive events like sprinting, throwing and jumping. What was known was that Mexico lay some seven and a half thousand feet above sea-level, hot and dry, and that any physical exertion at all would be difficult until our highly trained bodies had acclimatized. A chance to compete in Nairobi at an altitude of five and a half thousand feet would show up anything unusual in pole flexibility and run-up speed. It was an opportunity of a lifetime, and it had to be taken up in the lifetime of the opportunity, no matter how inconvenient.

Unfortunately, there was this slight problem of having one final exam paper on Philosophy at Queen's, and, of course as sod's law would have it, it was scheduled for the very day that I planned to be in Africa. There was only one person in the world who could solve my dilemma. He was the Professor of Logic and Metaphysics, who resided at No 9, University Square.

UNIVERSITY BLUES

Professor John Faris had seemed to me rather similar to all the other lecturers, readers, tutors, doctors and assorted exotically entitled academics of whom I had been much in awe at university; they were all somewhat removed from the real world. They certainly seemed far removed from my own vision of reality, distorted as it was by dreams of Olympic and sporting glory. There was, for example, my first philosophy tutor, an existentialist Frenchman by the name of François Bordet, who of course, would never have openly professed existentialism, for fear of committing the one cardinal sin of this creed, the dreaded 'bad faith' of living a life according to the dictates of any creed.

On the occasion of our very first tutorial the enigmatic François emerged amid a cloud of aromatic pipe smoke from behind a towering stack of books on his desk, which afforded only a fleeting glimpse of his mop of jet-black, long, wavy hair. As he reached the blackboard, his dark, heavy-lidded eyes slightly bulging out of an olive-hued, typically Gallic face, I fixed my gaze on the curved stem of his out-sized pipe and the leather elbow patches on his regulation tweed jacket, as his yellowish fingers traced with chalk and his impenetrable vowels annunciated the immortal legend;

Venus is the Morning Star
Venus is the Evening Star
The Morning Star is the Evening Star.

None of us in the tutorial had a clue as to what was going on here, this being after all our first day at university, nor did the subsequent discourse on the logic of syllogism and of argument by stipulation throw much light on the subject. I thought perhaps that I had stumbled into the wrong room. The funny thing is that nothing ever changed during my subsequent seven years at No. 9 as student, post-graduate and fellow professional philosopher – the wonderful François remained impenetrable right to the end, his untimely demise simultaneously bringing to an end both the essence and existence for which he had stood.

Professor Faris, on the other hand, would have shared precious little common intellectual ground with his continental colleague, being a typical product of the prevalent, rather more practical, tradition of British Empiricism. His acclaimed oeuvre included the definitive 'Truth Functional Logic' and an esteemed paper on the equivalence in meaning of the logical symbol 'hook' and the ordinary-language word 'entails' – as in, does 'p hook q' mean the same as 'p entails q'? Such pressing questions had occupied the professor's mind over a lifetime of study and teaching, so you can imagine that I was more than a little worried about his grasp of the concept of the effects of altitude on explosive physical performance. But I had to try!

Things did not look promising on the appointed day when a dusty dossier was unfolded on his desk, therein outlining all the philosophy department's previous requests from students asking to sit exams late. Injury, illness, bereavement, holidays and hangovers were all in there, even someone who wanted to take an Ethics paper on a different date because he had to go to a wedding… his own! All had been refused; "there is no precedent" the prof mused, his brain wrestling with at least six logical outcomes of the whole scenario.

His thick, milk-bottle pince-nez slipped a little further down on to the tip of that ski-slope proboscis and then he uttered that eternally optimistic word, "however".

It was enough to send my spirits soaring; and with good reason. Unknown to me, I had benefited from the vouchsafement of a heavyweight ally, namely the department's second-in-command and fervent sports enthusiast who was Reader in 'Social and Political Philosophy' at Queen's and was soon to become Professor of Politics at Durham, Alan Milne.

Dr Alan Milne, author of the definitive *Social Philosophy of English Idealism* had been blind since an exploding land-mine severed his optic nerve during a paratroop operation in the Second World War. He had subsequently completed his degree at the London School of Economics by dint of his wife and fellow students reading to him! At Queen's I was at first completely unaware of his disability, there being no clue in his strong stride and steady circumnavigation of stairs, chairs, doorways and rostrums, nor in the 'reading' of his lecture notes or frequent glancing at his wristwatch. Dr Milne's world was like a road map in his mind, except that with his calibre of mental ability there was the capacity to memorize absolutely everything. There was no need for hesitation. Plato's *Republic* was the thirty-seventh book from the right on the sixth shelf of his bookcase, the rostrum fifteen paces from the door, and so on. He was to become my research supervisor, inspiration, occasional jogging companion and friend.

I suppose that same kind of logical road map made it obvious to him that Kenya would be useful preparation for Mexico, that the Olympic Games were important, and that Queen's should help its first Olympic athlete by rescheduling an exam paper. At any rate Professor Faris was persuaded and two, sixteen foot long fibre-glass poles and myself were on our way to Nairobi.

LOST IN UGANDA

The events that ensued became part of athletics folklore. The small British team of six, including a manager who was primed to ensure the adequacy of African vaulting facilities, travelled out a few days ahead of me, leaving me to travel later on a huge East African Airways VC10 to Entebbe airport in neighbouring Uganda.

The voluptuous, but of uncertain age, blonde who had befriended me on board the long flight explained to me that the fourteen or so passengers going on to Nairobi would have to transfer at Entebbe on to a small turboprop plane. On first sight of it I noted that it could not have been much longer than my unusual baggage, the pole. However, the first sign of a problem arose when we observed the pilot of the smaller plane opening the cockpit window in an effort to accommodate the sixteen feet of fibre-glass being thrust in by two Ugandan baggage handlers.

"Do they fold in half?" "Are they collapsible?"

Other entry points were tried, but despite vigorous encouragement on the part of my buxom travelling companion, the lads simply could not get the poles on board. As the aircraft skimmed the roof-tops of the mud huts surrounding the airport on take-off, the last sight I caught of my valuable cargo was the two lads carrying the poles, end on end, off the tarmac to an uncertain destination.

Pole-less, I was met at Nairobi airport by the English-born Kenyan national Coach, John. My beautiful travelling companion, who was not backward coming forward, cadged a lift and told the enchanted coach all about how badly we had been treated and the saga of the disappearing poles. He told me not to worry and, rather optimistically I thought, insisted that they would turn up, but turn up they did, two days later and exactly one hour before the start of the competition. Not that it really mattered in the end because, as it turned out, there was no suitable vaulting facility at the national stadium. This was a great disappointment to me and to the spectators, especially in view of the fact that the local Minister for Sport had arranged for those poles to be transported from Entebbe by chartered jet. All the finely dressed ladies and their colonial consorts had to come to terms with cream tea in the tented viewing gallery without any entertainment from the Empire's first 16ft vaulter. Instead, I ran around the clay track that had made the legendary miler Kip Keino world famous. I stretched and I sprinted, but what I could not do was to take off and land in that concrete- paved sand dune.

The National Coach and the Minister for Sport saw me off at the airport, apologetically presenting me with two fabulous wood carvings for my trouble.

I had journeyed a round trip of twelve thousand miles for a rather less exalted form of experience than my mentors at No. 9 University Square had envisaged. I like to think that the late A. J. Milne would have understood, with typical stoicism, the value of such an episode to a blossoming Olympian, the complete indifference to pleasure and pain requisite to master vaulters. It certainly confirmed in me the growing suspicion that, as far as athletics is concerned, there are no utopias.

In case you think I'm making this up, what follows is an abstract from a Sunday Times series during the 2012 London Olympics in which several past Olympians were to recall their 'Best and Worst' memories. I was one of those chosen, as was Sheila Sherwood, silver medallist long jumper in Mexico:

> Which was your worst venue?
>
> That is easy. It was Nairobi in 1968. We went to the Kenyan national championships. I became the Kenyan 100ms champion. I lined up against these giggling little girls in bare feet. There was no proper run-up for the long jump pit. We had to be grateful, though because the British pole vaulter Mike Bull came across to compete and there was no pole vault pit. They spent the whole day digging a hole in the ground. A man with his wheelbarrow dumped sand for the pit but in the end it wasn't good enough. It was a wonderful trip, though.

GONE TO THE DOGS

The second incident which highlighted the glaring need for a re-evaluation of the equipment and facilities required by this increasingly dangerous event in the track and field calendar occurred a little closer to home. It is hard to overstate the prestige and historical standing of the White City Stadium, near Shepherd's Bush, within the world of athletics at that time. Crowds of 40,000 would regularly flock to the famous old arena on a summer week end throughout the fifties and sixties to watch Bannister and Landy, Gordon Pirrie, Chataway, Brasher and Zatopec and Kuts, Ron Clarke, Derek Ibbotson, John Pennel and all the international stars who competed in the oldest Championship in the world, the AAAs; or who represented their countries in the frequent international matches against the British national team. These matches have long since been

The 1968 N I championships at Paisley Park in Belfast saw me achieve the Olympic qualifying height with 16ft 2½in, the first outdoor 16ft vault by a British athlete.
It wouldn't have happened except for dad who not only was catching my pole on the day but had also arranged a lorry to bring the rubber conveyor belt I used for a run-up, the uprights, the crossbar, and the sacks for the landing pit from my self built shipyard training base. – but at least it was better than Kenya!

replaced by the ubiquitous Grand Prix, much to the detriment of the sport.

I had won the first of my thirteen AAA titles in 1966 (14 if you count my victory in a GB v. France international incorporating the 1973 AAA Decathlon, for which I was told my entry had been lost!) and again in 1967 and was determined to complete a hat-trick in the Olympic year of 1968, especially in view of the fact that my recent UK record of 16ft 2½in (4.95m) at Belfast's Paisley Park had catapulted me upwards into Europe's elite.

The vault pit at the White City had always been dangerous, but a freakish succession of two world records in 1963 by one of the all-time greats from the USA, John Pennel, who amazingly cleared 16ft 8in (5.09m) and 16ft 10in (5.13m) there, had made officialdom complacent. No effective improvements to the facility had been made, except for the introduction of a fork-lift truck to hoist the crossbar up to the new celestial heights of modern vaulting.

On the occasion of the 1968 Championships someone decided that there should be no pre-qualifying round on the Friday evening, leaving a record number of sixteen vaulters in the field to contest the final. Included in that field were three top Europeans, headed by the brilliant Italian, Renato Dionisi, a fast, rangy, goatee-bearded extrovert who just happened to be one of the very best exponents in the world of our chosen art.

Two things happened which led to farce. Firstly, the driver of the new fork-lift truck arrived at the stadium one hour late, which delayed the start of the event to 2:30 and in itself made completion of the final well-nigh impossible in the allotted time. Secondly, the officials in their wisdom decided to commence the jumping at the lowly height of just 13ft (4m) and, to accommodate the host of lesser vaulters which they had gratuitously admitted to the final, then made the fatal decision to progress the bar upwards at the alarmingly slow rate of 3in (7cm) at a time!

Caught in that harrier-mentality generated time-warp where 13ft jumps were considered respectable, officialdom had turned our event into a marathon that could not possibly be completed in one afternoon.

It was after 5pm before the three top Europeans and myself could start to think about taking our opening heights with the bar above 15ft (4.60m). Everyone else was finished vaulting, the scene set for a titanic battle, and at this point the fun really started!

The White City Stadium also doubled as a greyhound track on a Saturday evening and so by this time the dog-men started to arrive for their night of racing. As the men in white duster coats started setting up the traps and running the electric hare around the perimeter of the athletics track, the great British dog-race enthusiasts began arriving at the White City. They mixed uneasily with the many track and field stalwarts who had remained on the terraces, engrossed by the GB versus Italy battle for the AAA pole-vault championship. Tension and vaulters filled the air!

It is hard to believe that this was 1968 and not 1908! The stakes were high for two of Europe's top vaulters, namely Renato Dionisi, personal best of 17ft (5.20m), and me, personal best of 16ft 2½in (4.95m), a best I was improving almost every month. It all started getting interesting when the bar reached 15ft 6in (4.75m). I cleared easily on the first attempt, Dionisi also making it well with his compatriot Righi just squeezing over too.

The bar was now raised to 16ft (4.90m) and I again cleared comfortably first time of asking. The two Italians missed on their initial attempts. I was in the lead. Dionisi succeeded on his second attempt while Righi failed this and also his third and last try. The duel was on.

By this time, it was close to 7pm and the dog-men's patience had run out. They demanded that we leave the stadium. Our officials reluctantly conceded and ended the event, judging me the winner by virtue of that first-time clearance at 16ft. The Italian coach lodged a protest, quite rightly, and the officials then decided that the two of us come back the next morning, a Sunday, to finish the competition!

We didn't know what was going on, nor did anyone still watching, including the Athletics Press who were trying to file their copy for the Sunday newspapers. John Roberts wrote the definitive headline in the Express,

VAULT STAR SEES RED.

John wrote,

> Questions are likely to be asked today about why British pole-vault champion Mike Bull was forced to defend his A.A.A. title at London's White City before a group of irate greyhound officials and an electric hare.

So Dionisi, one of the most exciting and talented vaulters of the modern era, politely but firmly protested that he had other plans back in Milan the next day and so declined the generous offer of another day in Shepherd's Bush, insisting instead on his right to continue jumping.

Please try to remember that this was one of the world's most prestigious athletics championships. Here we were embroiled in the most unseemly and embarrassing row in front of a very hostile and unsympathetic crowd. All my worst childhood fears of ridicule came flooding back and I withdrew into myself. This mood of self-conscious introversion certainly did not help when the dog-men were persuaded to give us a half hour extension to resume and complete the contest.

The duel in the fading sun was resumed with the bar set at the new UK and Commonwealth record height of 16ft 6in (5.05m). It was one minute past seven when the great Dionisi slipped over a still wobbling bar.

I narrowly failed, just flicking the crossbar with an errant hand after what for me was technically the best jump I had done to date. So, after seven hours in the proverbial emotional wringer, I was relegated to second place with the dubious consolation (so it seemed at the time) of a big silver cup for best British performance of the championships and a guaranteed place on the Olympic team for Mexico. But you know what, I would gladly have swopped them both for that win.

These sorts of incidents, especially the one which became known as the 'Italian Job', received enormous publicity and certainly got the British Press on my side. I was portrayed as some sort of heroic pioneer – 'Your Actual Pioneer' as Neil Allen wrote in *The Times* – like an explorer on the edge of a vast and hostile wilderness. Without a doubt, the British public were already on my side. They loved the exciting, new event of fibre-glass vaulting and empathized with the athletic astronauts who defied gravity. Perhaps there was a sort of morbid fascination with the crash-and-burn danger of the event, a bit like motor sport; and the danger was real as evidenced by British International Dave Lease breaking a bone in his back at the notorious White City, and my own snapping of twelve poles mid- flight, resulting in a broken nose, thumb, wrist and ankle. But more than this, it was an aesthetically pleasing spectacle which seemed to combine power and grace. The analogy of Icarus is apposite, flight always giving way to a fall, success always ending in failure as the next height always wins in the end.

I was for many years Britain's leading pole-vault exponent in the pioneering era and my relentless fight for better facilities and equipment really seemed to capture everyone's imagination. It was in this particular leap year of 1968 that everyone's imagination was enhanced by a peculiarly quadrennial fever. Olympic fever was spreading like wild fire. But first there was a dream trip to Los Angeles in that crucial pre-Olympic season of 1967.

11. CALIFORNIA AND OTHER DREAMS

The decision to hold the 19th Olympiad at an altitude of four miles above sea-level was bizarre. The reasons are known only to the members of a self-perpetuating oligarchy, memorably described by writer Andrew Jennings in his eponymous book about the shady world of the International Olympic Committee, as the 'Lords of the Rings'.

The illuminati of this closed sporting circle, we are led to believe by Jennings, traded votes for university scholarships, junket-filled shopping extravaganzas and, dare one say, filthy money. Certainly, the choice of Mexico City, situated at a height of 7500ft was not made in the wider interests of the participating athletes.

It was known that there would be a drastically adverse effect on all endurance-based events, which meant all events beyond the running of 400m. Some prophets of doom even predicted that there would be deaths on the track, with lungs bursting and aortas exploding from oxygen deprivation. Chris Brasher, former Olympic Champion at 3000m steeplechase and famous pacemaker in Bannister's historic 4 minute mile, warned, "There will be those who will die".

Such fears might well have been warmly embraced by the likes of Al Oerter (USA), who had won one of his four gold medals wearing a surgical collar to prevent his discus throwing technique from snapping his neck. The greatest Olympian of all explained, "These are the Olympics. You die for them".

But Al's sentiments apart, the fear was that great champions like the USA's world mile record-holder, Jim Ryun, Australian 3-mile record-holder, Ron Clarke, and Britain's endurance men, like Bill Adcocks

Final Olympic trials, Portsmouth 1968. The new inflatable landing bed gave me the confidence to vault to a new UK and Commonwealth record of 16ft 7½in putting me into an exclusive club comprising the top 15 vaulters in the world. at the time

Photo; courtesy of Mark Shearman MBE

(marathon), Paul Nihill (20k walk), Ron Hill (10000m), Dick Taylor (5000m), Maurice Herriott (steeple) and John Whetton (1500m), would push themselves to a place beyond pain and human physiology. Would their indomitable spirit be defeated by rarefied air and their medals usurped by unknown mountain runners from Africa and South America?

The prophets of doom were almost right. Some prospective Olympians, however, had other problems on their mind.

CALIFORNIA DREAMING

Since returning to Belfast from Illinois in 1966 I had absolutely nowhere to train for vaulting. I continued to improve but all improvements in results were down to my ever-developing physical fitness, in terms of speed, strength and gymnastic ability, and owed nothing to refinements in technique. This state of affairs would have to change if I was to stand any chance of getting to an Olympic final.

In this most technical event I was largely unable to work on aspects of planting the pole, taking off, drive-in, rocking back and so on and therefore my personal best (ipso facto the UK record) improved by only 3in. in the year '66 to '67. There was simply nowhere suitable in Ireland to vault in either practice or competition, an unbelievable situation for a national champion in a major sport and one that most definitely cost irreparable damage to my technical development in future years. I was forced to treat representative competitions as opportunities to practice and to learn. One such opportunity followed my surprise silver medal at the 1966 Commonwealth Games in Jamaica, when I was selected to represent the Old Empire against the USA and the Soviet Union at the Los Angeles Olympic Stadium, in 1967, the height of the 'swinging sixties' and the beginning of 'Flower Power'.

The Commonwealth team stayed at the University of Southern California where I had a rare opportunity to train with and learn from the best athletes and coaches in the world. I remember the Southern California Coach, Vern Wolf, mentor to world record holder, Bob Seagren, telling me during one practice session that I had the potential to jump 17ft (5.20m). That comment alone made the trip worthwhile…

give a lad a dream! I was in my element, back in the sun and the superb vaulting facilities, all the time watching every move of the two current best vaulters on earth, Bob Seagren and Paul Wilson.

Wilson was the Mozart of the vault, a child prodigy who cleared 16ft (4.90m) at the age of 16 in an era when that height was truly world class. The only son of two Los Angeles doctors, he was tall and rather slender but blessed with the smoothest of running techniques. It was said you could place a cup of water on his head when he was sprinting down the runway, and he wouldn't spill a drop (I loved all this American bull).

He was never spotted at training during that trip, only occasionally around the campus in his electric blue Mustang sports car, looking every inch, with his deep tan and wrap-around sunglasses, the superstar he undoubtedly was. Paul was, however, destined to be something of a shooting star, burning brightly for only the briefest moment in time before disappearing into athletics oblivion.

On this occasion Wilson's star shone brilliantly. He won with a world-leading 17ft 5in (5.30m), only narrowly failing to break the universal record in one of the greatest virtuoso displays of fibre-glass vaulting ever seen. He demolished the classy field and stole the show from Jim Ryun, who, at the same time, was running the 1500m in a new world mark of 3:33.1. This was to be Wilson's last international appearance, at the age of 19.

The story goes that, in his relentless pursuit of perfection and with the prospect of Olympic glory ahead, the youthful Paul started experimenting with a high-protein diet. Perhaps the intention was to add some muscle to his surprisingly slight frame but, as it turned out, the effect was disastrous. Beset with recurring injuries and suffering constant muscle cramps, Wilson's short but truly spectacular career ended right there, with no major medals and no Olympic Games.

For me, it was back to the Queen's University playing fields and some more improvised running sessions. I had loved Southern California with its warm climate, the air scented with bougainvillea (smog permitting), the endless beaches… and the athletics tracks. I know it was an illusion but it seemed to me to be the mecca of track and field, with not only the L.A. Coliseum but magnificent tracks at Westwood, Mt Sac, Bakersfield, Santa Barbara, Fresno, Irvine and San Diego. They were all part of the sport's folklore, historical venues of the first sub-10second 100m, 60ft (18m) shot put, 200ft (60m) discus throw, 7ft (2.13m) high jump and so on – all landmarks which, as a youth, had fed my voracious appetite for sporting fairy tales.

A DESPERATE DIGRESSION

The Commonwealth v. USA meet was so successful that it was repeated in 1969 with the inclusion of a very strong Soviet team and so I could once again live out my childhood dreams. I was not the only athlete on this trip who was intoxicated by California. The big Russian vaulter, Gennady Bliznyetsov, the sixth best in the world who earned the sobriquet 'Desperate Dan' (after the comic book's heroic strongman who could eat a whole cow in a pie for dinner) because of his 6ft 4in, 16 stone (224lb) frame and granite-like features, was also being wooed, very perceptibly, by the wild West.

I had befriended Gennady the previous year at the White City when he had jumped a great national record, with my helping him by standing beside the runway throwing grass into the air to find him a good tail-wind (tail-winds help speed). I noticed then that he had reinforced the bottom end of his already monstrously heavy fibre pole with a 9 inch section of metal. This seemed odd to me in view of the fact that one of the great advantages of fibre poles over the old metal ones was their overall lightness. He duly explained to me, in an incongruously high pitched, falsetto voice, that the reinforced section would make the pole last longer because he had the habit of snapping the bottom 9in off the pole when he slammed it into the box. Talk about rugged!

Nothing much seemed to please Gennady, except vaulting high. The previous year, during the torrential rain-drenched qualifying round of the European Championships in Budapest, he had slipped down the pole three times in succession and thereby failed to reach the final. I myself, as an 18 year- old first-timer, jumped well to qualify for that final, vaulting in the rain being nothing unusual if you lived in Northern Ireland. Afterwards, in the athletes' canteen, I had been moved to offer condolences to my Russian friend but thought better of it when I saw his manic stare and the way he was attacking what might have been a whole cow-pie on his plate.

In Los Angeles, old 'Desperate' did vault well. His delight at this was, however, muted by traditional Soviet sang-froid, which made his visibly growing interest in the attractive American languages student who was acting as translator for their team, so much of a surprise. We were all pleased to see that the reputation of the gravity-defier's club was being upheld and we warmed to the sight of the two love-birds promenading hand in hand on the campus, sun-bathing on Venice Beach, listening to the Beach Boys and other decadent music, and generally behaving like any other two young West Coast lovers.

It was uplifting to all of us, except that is, to the KGB attaches who accompanied every Soviet team beyond the Iron Curtain. They were not at all uplifted by the behaviour of the man honoured with the title of 'Master of Sport' and, on returning home, publicly censured him and dropped him from the national team for displaying 'Un-Soviet-like' conduct. In their Marxist-Leninist myopia, they condemned their hero as a national disgrace.

I met old 'Desperate' again in 1991 during the World Masters Championships in Turku, Finland. On the training ground he looked as physically imperious as ever, lean and fit. We shook hands warmly and I complemented him on how good he looked (well, he was over 50), to which he replied in his peculiarly high-pitched voice,

"Only look good, Mike, only look good."

Shaking his head unhappily as he trudged back up the runway, pole in hand, he seemed hopeful, perhaps, that the course of nature could be reversed for just a moment to allow him one more great vault and, possibly, a final escape from Siberia to that Californian dream that had once been so close.

TOM MCAULEY AND THE BELFAST SHIPYARD

California would feature again in my quest for the Holy Grail, but first there was the immediate problem of finding a place to train at home in Belfast. That search had fate playing its hand in sport once again when, by chance, I met a charismatic personality on the Liverpool-Belfast ferry. The affable pipe smoker with the charisma was Tom McAuley, whose Celtic charm and velvet turn of phrase were hypnotic. I had been admiring this gleaming, black E-type Jaguar sports car in the ferry line-up when Tom emerged as the proud new owner and introduced himself as a former Queen's University and Northern Ireland pole-vault champion. Would I join him on board for dinner?

Over dinner Tom, an award-winning civil and structural engineer, listened with a brain attuned to building bridges to my usual pleading story about equipment and facilities. He, in turn, regaled me with stories about olden-day vaulting contests against his friend and then Irish vault champion, Ulick O'Connor, the famous Irish author, playwright and man about town.

Tom shared a measure of lyricism with his illustrious friend, so it wasn't a surprise when he mused that surely, we can find a hall or build a shed to train in. With the requirements of a hall 50m in length and 10m in height agreed between us, Tom, all the time concentrating on the finely cantilevered sweep of his pipe, said that he would be in touch. I privately remembered that I had heard that one before, as I watched the aesthetically pleasing silhouette of the E-type roaring off down the ferry ramp.

One day and one phone call later, I was inspecting the large, glass-roofed upper floor of a disused timber shed owned by Harland and Wolff Shipyard, courtesy of one Tom McAuley. Tom had contacted a friend, Dennis Rebeck, who just happened to be the boss of Harland & Wolff! It was perfect; hundreds of metres of concrete floor and a sky-high glazed roof which permitted the winter sun to warm the interior to a level which would facilitate the flexing of fibre-glass poles. All it needed was a raised, wooden runway 141ft 6in long and some sort of landing area.

Tom supplied the former with a delivery at my new base of 8ft x 4ft plywood panels and dozens of solid, 8in x 2in timber planks. My father and I spent the next couple of days nailing the panels on to the 8-inch-high planks to form a 140ft long runway. We carefully cut a wedge out of the final panel to accommodate the 8-inch-deep box into which the pole is planted at take-off. At the other end of the runway a large stair-well opened up a 30-foot drop to the ground floor; so, to give me

*My self built training facility at the shipyard.
Anti clockwise from top left : takeoff, clearance and landing all encouraged by a willing band of helpers from the shipyard on their lunch break.*

the full measure of my run-up, we had to project the end panel about one metre out over the edge of this drop. This made the first steps of the run-up rather hairy, with the sheer drop to the concrete below and the board panel bouncing like a diving platform under my weight. I figured, 'What the hell, it is a dangerous event'.

The landing area was more difficult. The American portable style of compressed foam rubber wedges were financially out of the question at a cost of over a thousand dollars. Then one of the shipyard workers, who were increasingly fascinated at the goings-on in the old shed, suggested that he might be able to lay hands on some discarded bunk mattresses from a ship in dock for a refit. A short time later, the sudden appearance of 20 old, straw-stuffed mattresses confirmed my suspicion that many hands had obviously been recruited to the 'Save Mike' campaign and I had a firm foundation for my landings.

To complete the area a detailed inspection of the 'Yellow Pages' under the listings for upholsterers led me down many dark, dead ending alley-ways in search of scrap foam rubber to place on top of the mattresses. One of those alleys led me to the door of Eric Moffett's upholstery factory, and I hit the jackpot. Eric was a sports fan and did everything to ensure that I got as much foam as I needed. I procured some large, hessian sacks used for transporting potatoes and stuffed them with the scraps of foam. The vaulting area was now complete.

From October 1967 I started jumping every day, trying to make up for lost time, fitting in sessions between university lectures. I installed my old barbell and weights in one corner for thrice weekly strength sessions and there was plenty of room on the concourse for sprinting, while that notorious stair-well served ideally for power running up and down the steps. The raised, plywood runway was surprisingly fast, especially after we procured a broken rubber conveyor belt from the Craigantlet quarry and laid it on top of the plywood; the improvised landing area was soft and safe as long as you did not fall into the cracks between the sacks, and there were dozens of technical helpers on hand every session.

Who said the Shipyard was a sectarian hotbed? My new helpers were the dock-side workers who came to watch the lunchtime training sessions, and, within a few days, I had a squad of specially trained pole catchers, run-up check-mark watchers, take-off point observers and assorted cheer-leaders. Some days there was perhaps a crowd of fifty, including Tom, who was growing more and more interested in the double-pendulum mechanics of the pole-vault and the lad from Belfast trying to master them.

The result was spectacular. It was as if the genie had been let out of the bottle. After 18 months of virtual stagnation, early in 1968 I set three successive British indoor records at Cosford between January and March, culminating in that first milestone clearance of 16ft 1¾in (4.93m). By June I had cleared a world-class 16ft 6in (5.05m) in a dockside session filmed by the BBC. The media were getting a hold on the 'boys-own' story of a young vaulter in Northern Ireland training for the Mexico Olympics in a shipyard shed with an army of cloth-capped dockers for technical support. Sports photographers and journalists from all over the country were regular visitors to my thunderdome as I inched closer to the magical 17ft (5.20m) mark, and potential Olympic glory.

SPORTSNIGHT WITH COLEMAN

An important step on the road to Mexico was, for me, the staging of a Wednesday evening meet at Crystal Palace in early September '68 to give the already selected Olympic squad some much-needed competition. At my shipyard base I had been training like a man-possessed all summer under the watchful eyes of Tom and my father. I had achieved competitive victories over opposition from Poland, Germany, Switzerland, Canada, France and had avenged the 'Italian Job' with a win over Dionisi at

Crystal Palace. All I needed for a good, confidence-boosting send-off was an official clearance of that elusive five metres. This was to be my night.

It was also an important night for BBC sports presenter, David Coleman, as he was launching the first programme in his new series, Sports Night with Coleman, live from Crystal Palace. I cleared a new UK record of 16ft 6¼in (5.04m) which was not only the highlight of the evening's Athletics, but perfectly timed to be viewed live on prime-time television and provide a glorious scoop for Coleman's new show.

I was interviewed by a delighted David after the competition in the impromptu studio at the Palace and was able to watch and offer critical analysis of my vault on the taped replay.

I candidly pointed out to David lots of little mistakes in my form that would have to be worked on. David Coleman and the nation were now fully behind my mission to Mexico.

HUBRIS AND NEMESIS IN SPORT

Two days after my Sportsnight success the team was in Portsmouth for the traditional send-off match between the full Olympic squad and 'The Rest'. Experience forewarned me of the notoriously bad on-shore wind (headwind), the slow run-up and poor landing area at the seaside track, so I was less than optimistic about a good result. It was therefore a pleasant surprise to find a favourable wind and a brand-new inflatable landing pit in the form of a series of cigar-shaped rubber tubes inside a huge, rubberized envelope. A sports equipment scientist in the Isle of Wight had responded to my constant nagging in the press about bad facilities by inventing a new, self-sealing, inflatable landing pit. My campaign for better and safer equipment was paying dividends at last.

I responded in the best way possible with another UK and Commonwealth record of 16ft 7½in (5.08m) and leaped into the world's top 15 ranking list at just the right time. Furthermore, as a measure of their support for me, the British Athletics Board gave me the new pit to take home to my shed. After many hours of manually squeezing the air out of every tube, I folded the whole giant package up and put it into the back of the team bus. My 'portable' pit weighed about a quarter of a ton and eventually had to be shipped to Belfast… but it was mightily appreciated.

Greek tragedy teaches that boastfulness and over-confidence, which was called 'hubris', would offend the Gods and be punished by an inescapable downfall, called 'nemesis'.

I was not boastful by nature or overly confident, St Malachy's College schooling and living in Northern Ireland saw to that. But by way of ironic postscript, it was about a week later during my final shipyard training session before leaving for Mexico that I landed awkwardly on the new airbed, my knees jack-knifing into my face, breaking my nose and knocking myself unconscious. On departure for the Games my team-mates kindly reassured me that the colour of my eye sockets coordinated well with the blue and red of our Hardy Amies designed uniform. I didn't mind. Hubris and nemesis could take their best shot. I was on that plane to the Games.

12. MEXICO 1968

It has been said that Mexico was the last 'true' Games; no drugs, no politics, no illicit payments, which is really what most people generally mean when they use the word 'true' in this context. Sorry to disappoint but on this definition there has never been a 'true games', and Mexico was no exception. There has always been politics in the Olympics. In Mexico only one thing had a greater impact than Bob Beamon's extraordinary long

In our Hardy Amies Olympic suits Left to Right: Dick Taylor (5000m), Lynn Davies (long jump olympic defending champion and myself sporting a broken nose.

jump, and that was the political protest by Tommy Smith and John Carlos, gold and bronze medalists in the 200ms. Their raised, gloved clench-fisted salute with heads bowed during their national anthem hit the world of sport like a bombshell. Their protest for human rights equality was really the Black Lives Matter of that era. Incidentally, Australian Peter Norman won silver and decided to support Smith and Carlos by wearing on his tracksuit their Olympic Project For Human Rights badge. But Carlos had forgotten his black gloves and so Norman suggested they wear one glove each – hence that iconic image on the podium. No good came of this. Smith and Carlos were kicked out of the Village and suspended by the US Olympic Committee, while Norman had blotted his copybook enough to be omitted from Australia's Munich Olympic team despite being a shoo-in. In 2012 The Australian government apologized for the treatment he had received in his home country. Norman sadly died in 2006. Smith and Carlos were pallbearers at his funeral, friends forever in death as well as life.

However, there have always been two other evils in Olympic sport.

DRUGS AND DOUGH

Mexico heralded the first systematic dope testing programme. The result was one positive test! Yes, one positive and it was for an illegal alcohol level! As for dough, who knows; shoe money did exist but I did wonder at high-profile USA athletes who were wearing one famous brand of sports shoe on one foot and a rival brand on the other? Just a bit eccentric I suppose?

If you are doing a sports story these days the related subjects of illicit payments and doping cannot be avoided. I'm not sure how close I came to either in the sixty's and seventies.

With the former, my expenses claim form in respect of travelling from Belfast to London for an early GB International was found by the Hon. Treasurer of the British Board to contain payment for a tuna sandwich. The 5 shillings requested was denied as being surplus to need. It is worth noting that the said Treasurer was one Harold Abrahams, the estimable 1924 Olympic 100m Champion of *Chariots Of Fire* fame. Harold and I got on really well after this during my long career, but it is worth noting that his own Olympic preparations were censured by the authorities back then when he hired professional sprint coach Sam Mussabini to train him. It smacked of filthy professionalism and stood against good old British Corinthian amateurism. But I reckon he was quite entitled to hire old Sam; after all, his great sprint rival, Scot Eric Liddell who eventually withdrew from that epic 100ms in Paris because it was held on a Sunday, went on to win gold in the 400ms – as Dylan would say– "with God on his side." Harold was a truly inspirational athlete for many of us. He presented Lynn Davies with a personally inscribed watch on the occasion of his first 26ft (8ms) long jump. He told me that when I cracked the magic 16ft (4.90m) barrier I too would get one. If you should get to read this Harold, you owe me a watch?

In truth, the attitude toward payments in many so-called amateur sports, not just Olympic sports, was rapidly changing due to an all-pervasive commercial expansion. Athletics was at the forefront of this; throughout Europe, from Scandinavia to France and Italy, there was really a covert recognition that top athletes get paid. In Milan in 1968, when I was emerging as a world class vaulter, I found myself in the winner's spot on the podium with a medal in one hand and a brown envelope in the other. The envelope contained £100 in lira, small-fry really, but at a time when the 'A' in AAAs and IAAF (International Amateur Athletics Federation) stood for 'Amateur', strictly against the rules.

Shoe money in track and field and boot money in rugby, where the manufacturer paid a sportsman to wear their branded footwear and gear, was prevalent well before 1968. Official response to all this commercial enterprise was to insist that branded stripes and logos be covered up with tape. The futility of this was evident when rain would cause the tape to fall off! All this sort of hypocrisy was only 50 years after the authorities banned and stripped of medals the 1912 Stockholm Olympic Decathlon and Pentathlon Champion, Native American Jim Thorpe, who had been guilty of being paid $50 for playing a baseball game earlier. "You are truly the greatest athlete in the world" the King of Sweden had said when placing the gold medal around the quiet giant's neck. Jim replied "Thanks King" and walked off. His family were presented with his medal long after his passing and a statue was erected.

It was also just a few years before Zola Budd and Mary Decker were paid a reported fee of £90,000 each to rerun their Olympic debacle at London's Crystal Palace.

As for doping, I had early experience with a mental stimulant while an undergraduate at Queen's University. It was called Pro Plus, a strong caffeine tablet that saw me through a few all night study sessions at exam time. It also fuelled a few athletic competitions at the time. I don't know if it put me over the legal caffeine limit because I was never tested in that era. There was no testing then!

Some think that doping in sport began with Ben Johnson. The world watched in awe as the massively muscular Canadian literally jumped out of the blocks in the 1988 Seoul Olympic 100ms, demolishing the invincible Carl Lewis in a world record 9.7sec. The next day he was disqualified for taking a banned anabolic steroid.

However it didn't start there. Some readers more stricken in years might go all the way back to the 1967 Tour de France and that near vertical ascent up Mont Ventoux in temperatures exceeding 50°C. Britain's Tommy Simpson, a world champion and Olympic medallist, was suffering from stomach cramps and diarrhoea and was advised to quit the peloton. He didn't quit. Zigzagging deliriously to a stop, he fell to the road but told his mechanic, "On, on, on". After a few more meters he fell again, unconscious, hands locked to his handlebars. Pronounced dead in a nearby hospital, the clues were in the pocket of his jersey, a half full tube of amphetamines and two empties, which he had been washing down with brandy during the race. It was common practice in pro cycling at the time.

It's still not the start, not by a long way. Back in 1936, with Hitler's notorious Berlin Games in mind, Nazi medics were testing anabolic steroids on prisoners. Perhaps this partly explains German's unexpected success in the throws?

Further back in the annals of time, one marathon runner in the 1904 St Louis Games called Thomas Hicks narrowly avoided death after an overdose of brandy and strychnine. A commentator at the time also referred to the common practice of imbibing caffeine, cocaine and heroin!

But you have to go back to ancient Greece to find the origins of performance enhancing supplements. Galen, physician and writer whose work influenced medicine for centuries, advocated 'rear hoof of Abyssinian ass, ground up, boiled in oil and flavoured with rose hip and petals' to improve the performance of Pankration[1] competitors in the ancient Olympics of the 7th century BC.

Herbal medicines and hallucinogens from an array of fungi, along with bread stuffed with opium from poppies, all used by these gladiatorial forebears in this most popular Olympic event where a mixture of boxing and wrestling without rules often only ended in the death of the loser. Not unlike the Tour de France then? There was also lots of money and status for the winners.

As for my own experience of all this, the Sixties may have been swinging in London but in British athletics we were as naive as lambs to the slaughter. This era saw the erecting of the Berlin Wall and the drawing of the Iron Curtain. It was all about global power politics, East versus West, Communism versus Democracy, and sport was the vital pawn in the bigger game of which social system was better.

The USSR, GDR, the entire Eastern block all put sport at the forefront of government support. One of my first internationals was against the USSR and I jumped a personal best height in finishing 2nd to the Soviet champion. I was an 18 years old student living on a meager grant. He was a 25 years old army officer, a Master of Sport who had no duties other than training, food and a flat free gratis (yes that Russian Gennady again!). It was common knowledge he and the entire team were on a State performance enhancement programme, willing or not.

I knew all this but I still viewed him as a hero, a great athlete and I envied his success. Another hero of mine was an East German who was to become Olympic Champion and world record holder. In 2012 before London's Olympics the Sunday Times did an article on past Olympians, called *Best and Worst*, and I was asked who was the best competitor I had faced. I gave the German's name immediately. He was an Olympic Champion, a World Record Holder, virtually unbeaten over 6 years. But I knew he was part of the State doping programme, he had to be, no choice if he wanted to keep his passport and jet-set lifestyle. It surprises me that he was my pick. Shouldn't I have resented the cheating, the unfairness of it all?

---

1 a modified fight to the death

Probably. On the other hand, I had choice. And I had the new athletes grant of £10 per month to look forward to. We were the Great Britain Team and we were amateurs. I'll illustrate with a true story. I had befriended Olympic long jump Champion Lynn Davies prior to the 1968 Mexico Games. I had climbed the world rankings all season, thanks to my new Belfast Shipyard vaulting base, and NI Athletics decided to run an international event at Paisley Park Track and to showcase two events, men's long jump with Lynn and Pole vault with an American opponent for me.

Lynn and his wife Meriel came over to stay at my parents house in North Belfast. During the stay we were approached by local health food shop owner and well known endurance swimmer Jack McClelland. He told us a health food company wanted us to accept sponsorship from them to promote a product called Biostrath. It was a heady mixture of honey, malt and wheatgerm. Our payment was free supply of Biostrath up to the Olympics. We agonised over this and kept it mostly a secret, fearful of contravening our amateur status! What would Galen have made of this? Or our Soviet, American and European counterparts who were being paid to train and compete, and who were, for the most part, drugged up to the eyeballs?

That may or may not have been true, but what was certain to us was the simple fact that the thinner air offered less wind resistance to sprinters and jumpers and that our fast-twitch muscles reacted better in the sun and intense heat. Once we had gone past the normal first stages of breathlessness in training (after only jogging one lap of the track), we were really flying. I managed a second and a third place with respectable 5m vaults in pre-Games meets. Our individual preparations were reaching fever pitch with my training partner, reigning Olympic long-jump champion Lynn Davies, chanting his daily mantra, "Bigger, better and browner, every day!"

Lynn and I worked according to a training schedule which rotated jumping, sprinting and lifting weights on an ongoing three- day cycle. We were in Mexico for some six weeks and therefore we were really getting into tremendous shape. One day a week was a rest-day, for swimming, sun-bathing, sight-seeing and, on one memorable occasion, for taking up a rather unusual invitation.

An Unusual Invitation

At the athlete's village, Lynn and I met this very attractive Mexican lady who was working there as an aide and, in the course of a casual conversation, she intimated that she was a hypnotherapist and would love to help us with some relaxation therapy. My Welsh friend was a long-term insomniac, whose only rapid-eye movement (the hallmark of deep sleep) in all the years I have known him could be induced by the long-limbed blonde who happened to be his wife, the beatific Meriel. However, Lynn did have the added pressure of defending his title against the threat of Bob Beamon. In any case, our new friendly analyst thought we were both wound up far too tightly for our own good and invited us to her home to unwind a little.

My mother, Anne McKee from County Armagh, was a gregarious and unfailingly optimistic red-head who was always likened to Lucille Ball's dizzy character in the popular television series of the era, *I Love Lucy*. She had instilled in me the Orchard County attitude that every door unopened is an opportunity missed. No invitation should be eschewed, certainly not one from a dark-eyed Latino promising a sporting elixir. I urged that we accept the invitation.

The rambling, Spanish style villa with its white-washed arches and red, terracotta tiles was set in luxurious gardens in the heart of one of the more affluent suburbs of the great city. Our charming hostess offered us ice cold orange juice after our hot and scary taxi ride across the bustling city and ushered us into the quiet of the garden. We were beckoned to lie down on two mats laid out beside a bubbling waterfall and, barely able to contain our excitement at the unfolding adventure on the lawn, we willingly obliged. The ensuing, heavily accented dialogue went something like this;

"Lie back and close your eyes… breathe easily, in through your nose and gently out through the mouth."

At this early stage I was already in trouble, not because the session was by now obviously going to be a genuine attempt at therapy, but because my recently broken nose still did not allow sufficient air to travel up it to prevent suffocation.

"Relax your whole body... start with the toes and slowly up to the legs... relax the lower back, the abdomen... loosen the shoulders, the arms... now the neck and jaw. Think of pebbles in the stream... you are a pebble, rolling gently downstream... you are sleepy... rolling closer to the waterfall... gently tumbling down, falling, falling..."

By this time, I was not so much sleepy as drowning in the suffocating effort of trying to breathe through a blocked nose and the baked desert that passed for my mouth. Lynn was very quiet, quite obviously tranquillized in a dream of rolling stones;

"You are very relaxed... now you are in a deep sleep... roll over and totally relax."

This was the crunch. Lynn was supposedly hypnotized but, because of the angle of our prostrate bodies, I could not see if he had rolled over as directed. He probably had, I thought to myself, and in any case I did not want to offend our hostess. I dutifully rolled over and, pretending to be in a hypnotic trance as I did so, became gradually aware of my fellow subject's body shaking and then bursting into unrestrained laughter. As the dirty dog apologized for not being a good subject I realized that I had to go on alone with the charade. As we all know, that kind of shaking laughter is highly infectious and I almost sustained a hernia trying to contain myself. I deserved a gold medal right there for that performance.

Thanking our hostess we hit the street in an explosion of uninhibited laughter which, tears streaming from our eyes, lasted the entire taxi ride back to the village. If the object of the exercise was relaxation, then, mission accomplished.

THE OLYMPIC VILLAGE

The Olympic Village itself was a huge, enclosed area of apartment blocks, restaurants and training facilities. In the Spartan apartments we were billeted two to a room, with no TV and no personal stereos. After a typical day's training there really was not much to do. The lads became particularly creative at trying to relieve the boredom; thus was born, the famous 'grid game'. Telescopes installed on the different floors of our block were trained on the segregated female quarters, the windows of which had been assigned a sort of geographic grid reference which everyone quickly learned. The shout would go out, "B4!", and all the scopes would reel into position to focus on the slightest glimpse of any female, or part thereof, in the forbidden zone. Ah! The age of innocence.

Pre games meeting held in the olympic village where I finished second to Isaksson

The restaurants were open 24/7, as they say, and catered lavishly for all tastes and all cultures. There was so much food that the coaches of the emerging nations (and of some that were fully emerged) would have to stand at the end of the self-service line and unload the trays full of steaks, eggs, pasta, cakes and ice-cream; their light-weights were in danger of turning into super-heavies.

One sight never to be forgotten was that of the giant Soviet weight-lifter, Leonid Zabotinsky, at breakfast one morning. Looking down from his height of almost two metres, this giant could not really have had a view of anything below the massive girth of his waistline, and his ambling, backward-leaning gait only served to emphasize the infinite circumference of what passed for his neck. The trays in both his hands buckled under the weight of a dozen eggs, a kilo of bacon, three large steaks, a dozen buttered rolls, four litres of milk and God knows how many assorted yoghurts, bananas and apples. Every measured, waddling footstep looked to be in slow motion and cumbersome in the extreme... that is until big Leonid got on to the lifting platform. Then he became 26 stone of greased lightning, explosively lifting a world record as well as the gold medal.

The moral dilemma for the philosopher was the waste. The food thrown away every day would have fed the half million starving citizens who lived in tin shacks in the shanty town just across the main highway from the village. Students who dared to protest at such injustices by staging a rally in the main square of the city were unceremoniously machine-gunned to death in their hundreds by security forces. The security forces were nervous of the prying eyes of Western journalists, like British athletics correspondent John Rodda, who was pinned to the ground of his hotel room balcony overlooking the student protest, a gun pressed to his head and held there in that terrifying position for hours. John's hair turned white overnight. No terrorism? No politics? Ask the sports journalist, John Rodda, who witnessed this first hand.

Back at the politically sanitized Village, the training facilities were a dream. There was a full international size rubber 'Tartan' track with two great vaulting areas. Among the many unforgettable sights witnessed on that training track were the revolutionary backwards-leaning high-jumping of unknown American student, Dick Fosbury, and the extraordinary spear- chucking of the legendary 'Mr Javelin', Janis Lusis of the soviet Union.

The practice area for javelin adjoining the track allowed for a throwing distance of well over 100m, in excess of the world record. It did not, however, allow for the novel training methods of Lusis. He was working on arm speed the day that British javelin champion, Dave Travis, and myself stopped to watch. Lusis had started throwing the much smaller, lighter women's javelins and Dave, a great student of sport in general and spear-throwing in particular, explained that he was doing this in order to get an 'over-speed' transfer into his action whenever he turned his attention to the heavier men's model.

The effect was utterly mind-altering. At the far end of the throwing area the ground rose into a rocky out-crop about 30 or 40ft high, forming a natural boundary for the landing javelins' danger zone. We watched in amazement the blur of explosive force from Lusis's launching pad as the powerful athlete propelled the missile high up into the blue sky, where it disappeared for many seconds only ended by a puff of dust and clay as the javelin landed half-way up the rock face. He repeated it again and again, higher and higher up that rock face.

Speechless, Dave later paced out the rough distance and estimated an incredible 330ft. (100ms), the equivalent of one football goalmouth to the other. I had to help Dave back to our room and put him in a nice, quiet, darkened area. As for Mr Javelin, he went on to win the gold, one of three consecutively in the event.

THE GAMES

The Games themselves produced the expected feast of superlative athletics with world records in 15 different events. Four sprinters equalled the World Record in the men's 100m, with the USA's Jim Hines breaking it with 9.9sec to win the final. Wyomia Tyus did the same in the women's 100m with 11sec. The other World Record performances came in the women's 200m, 4 x 100m, long-jump and shot, and the men's 200m, 400m, 800m, 4 x 100m, 4 x 400m, 400m hurdles (David Hemery, with Britain's only gold), long-jump, triple-jump and pole-vault (equal). There were no deaths but note the absence of any distance events in the roll of honour. Ron Clarke, Jim Ryun, Ron Hill, Paul Nihill, Maurice Herriott and Noel Carroll were among the casualties of altitude that I witnessed in near life-threatening distress on crossing the finish line. There were many others.

THAT JUMP

The jumping events were amazing… and then there was Beamon. Dave Travis, myself and some of the lads positioned ourselves low down in the stand near the long-jump pit so that we could give Lynn some audible support. Bob Beamon of the USA, who had only qualified for the final on his final attempt, by stuttering and almost stopping at take-off to record a distance of almost 27ft (8.23m), was on the runway. A tall, slender black cat with the speed of a cheetah, he dipped slightly and hit the board perfectly, probably for the first time in his life, and recorded the first actual jump of the final.

Many times since, I have closed my eyes and tried to recapture the historic feat I had seen. He ran very quickly, an impression of unbridled speed, even in this company of very quick athletes. He went very high, higher even than the measuring rail alongside the sand, and seemed to hang for an eternity in the air before hitting the sand. He landed almost at the end of the pit and immediately rebounded out on to the track, doing a series of bunny-hops as if he had not yet expended all his momentum. The judge moved the optical measuring device along the rail until it fell off, still miles short of the footprints left in the sand. An old-fashioned steel tape was summoned and, a full 20 minutes later, the measurement went up on the board… 8.90m!

Lynn, along with all the other jumpers, had been wandering around for those 20 minutes, looking lost, looking as though the event had been cancelled. It virtually had. Beamon, meanwhile, was behaving like a man intoxicated, falling at the feet of his team-mate and mentor and giving thanks to the great former champion, Ralf Boston. Lynn shouted up at us, "How far is it?" Dave's conversion tables for the event, which we used in those days to get our feet and inches, stopped at 8.50m (28ft).

"It's over 28ft.," I shouted back, knowing that no human had ever gone that far before. But a better mathematician behind me, in the form of Bruce Tulloh, had worked it out exactly; "It's 29ft 2in."

Game over… for the next 24 years actually! The rain and thunder which followed didn't change anything; it was simply Zeus, King of all gods on Mount Olympus, admitting a very special mortal through their Celestial Gates.

The last thing I heard of Beamon he was living in Florida, working with youth in sport. A few years ago, he invited the man he had succeeded as champion, Lynn Davies, out to Miami to give a talk. They met at Miami Airport for the first time in 30 years. On seeing Lynn, big Bob took a running jump along the concourse and leaped up to touch the ceiling, declaring, "I can still jump!"

THE VAULT

In my own event the world was treated to the greatest pole-vault competition in history, and one of the longest. The final started promptly at 12:30 and the last jump was taken at 7:52. If you consider that we checked in for the event at 11 am, the short, explosive sport of pole-vaulting was in reality a 9 hour marathon. Three men equalled the global record of 17ft 8¾in, with the USA's Bob Seagren winning on count-back to preserve his nation's unbroken run of Olympic victories. His team-mate, the great John Pennel, also cleared the winning height but was denied the jump by the rule which disallowed the pole to pass under the crossbar on release. That rule had already been rescinded by the international federation, being unfair (and stupid) but the new rules did not take effect until after the Games. Shown the red flag, old John sank down on to the bench beside me, put his head in his hands and wept. At the age of 28 he knew there would not be another chance of Olympic glory (yes, 30 was considered 'old' for sport in those days).

I did well to reach the final. From an official report;

> There were several very disturbing delays during the competition. With the bar at 5.10m (16ft 8¾in), the officials took fully 5 minutes to re-measure before Bull's first attempt; then after Engle had cleared at the second attempt, some marks were discovered on the runway and the officials ordered them to be washed off -Malyutin and Bull were kept waiting 10 minutes for their last attempts…

> …Mike Bull should be touring the continent to vault against the really good heights. There is little wrong with his technique but it must be exposed to a great deal of hard competition, not vaulting each month against his own British record; this is still some 13in below the best in the world. His final place in Mexico was a great achievement and one that should help his confidence for Munich.

THE CLIFF DIVE

A note of pathos closes the Mexico chapter. After the intensity of the Games, we were all taken for a week's holiday to a beach-side hotel in the millionaire's resort of Acapulco. It was paradise, jogging on the beach in the sun and surf and formulating grand plans for our sporting future. One trip took us to the famous cliff divers of Acapulco. I was spellbound at the sight of a figure some 130ft high above us standing on a tiny cliff-top shelf. To add to the dramatic effect, lightning forked in the background as the diver arched himself into a narrow gorge below that had about two inches of water and projecting rocks. As he plunged to certain death the tide rushed in to fill the gorge and the human bullet punched a life-saving hole in the surf to complete his dive. We made our way out through the dark, narrow caves to the street entrance where a sorry sight met our eyes. The diver, who had just performed a truly Olympian feat of Herculean dimensions, was sitting on the stone floor with his wife and several tiny children beside him begging for spare coins! He must have been 50 years of age. I wish John Pennel had been there! He would have tried that dive.

13. DAVID AND GOLIATH

There it was, right enough, towering 150ft above the housing rows of East Belfast, Goliath! In the very spot where my timber-shed training base used to be.

The whole Mexico experience had been profoundly motivating for this young athlete. I returned to university in Belfast inspired and ready to train harder than ever for the next big one, the European Championships to be held in Athens in 9 months time. However, all my plans were dashed on learning that my beloved shipyard shed had been demolished while I was thousands of miles away at the Olympics. Now, in its place stood the largest crane in the world, called Goliath. Back to square one, nowhere to train. Goliath represented the 'system' that had persistently failed the specialist athlete and, in the unfair world of sports provision, reversed legend and defeated its David, me!

NORDWIG

This really could not have happened at a worse time in an athlete's career. I had learned so much at the Games, rubbing shoulders with the greatest athletes on the planet and discovering all the little nuances that made them great. I had watched Wolfgang Nordwig, the precision engineer from Jena in East Germany, who had won the bronze medal and a share in that world record, practice alone with great precision with his personal coach on a deserted training track outside the Village.

The bar was set high, very high, and the German would take a vault and then sit down in the shade for half an hour and just sort of relax.

This went on for a couple of hours. I had never seen anything like it before. By comparison, everything in my own jumping sessions seemed so frenetic; a thorough one hour warm-up of jogging, stretching and striding and short-approach vaulting, followed by vault after vault, with little rest in between, in a sort of increasing frenzy of excitement at doing something that I was really enjoying.

Not Wolfgang. No emotion of any sort was displayed, no obvious joy at clearing these fantastic heights, very little discussion with his coach, but lots of sitting down and conservation of energy and, apparently, lots of thought and concentration – they call it 'focus' today. Can you think of a better way of preparing for an eight hour final where he was to be called upon to vault about once an hour? I resolved to be more patient, less emotional, more self-contained, more like Nordwig, who was to go on to become Olympic Champion and World Record holder.

SCHIPROWSKI

Then there was the West German phenomenon, Claus Schiprowski, who had taken the silver medal with an unprecedented succession of five personal bests, ending in a share of the Olympic record at 5.40m. He was only 5ft 8in tall but had fantastic speed on the runway, a bit like Jonathan Edwards, Britain's World Record triple-jumper, in looking so quick as to be almost out of control. This speed enabled Claus to grip very high on the pole and to use a very strong 'flex' pole for more whip. Also, when he drove forward and upwards into the bending implement, he employed the fastest leg-lift I had ever seen. The whipping limbs on a strong pole shot his body high up off the end in an uncontrollable spiral and, in fact, he frequently looked out of control when clearing the bar. His jump at the record height saw his body slide sideways, parallel to the crossbar as he cleared.

I became quite friendly with the good-natured German and asked him about his leg-whip technique. He told me he practiced daily for hours on the high-bar, used in gymnastics, and that with various ankle weights strapped to his feet and would repeat that fast leg shoot over and over. This was a must for my future training. Later on, as a guest at the Birmingham International indoor meet, I heard from Germany's world indoor champion, Tim Lobinger, that Claus has fallen on hard times. I hope he comes through them… and, if he ever reads this, I happen to know a nice little beach in Andalucia with a good vaulting pit not far away. He would always be welcome.

SEAGREN

There was also the man himself, Bob Seagren, the Olympic Champion, who was quite simply the best of his era. A typical Californian extrovert and set in the self-confident mould of vaulting greats Warmerdam, Richards, Bragg and Hansen, he and his brother Art had been vaulting since the age of eight. They surfed and board-skated (in the hand-stand position!) and, like everyone in Los Angeles wanted to be 'an actor'. He may well have been a dead ringer for film-star Robert Culp (*Bob and Carol* and *Ted and Alice*) but Robert Seagren developed into one hell of an athlete while a student at the University of Southern California.

Seagren had a very distinctive running style, a high knee-lift almost prancing action, and was very dynamic on the pole, his body retaining great tension when others (like me) would let their legs drop and flop into a bad, jack-knife position over the crossbar. Nowadays this body tension is the aim of the all-important 'core stability'. In the future I would try to keep my body shape straighter for longer.

I got to know Bob as well as possible, given all the hangers-on and athletics 'wanabees' that surrounded him, being his guest at the London Playboy Club once (how Hollywood is that?) and sharing the odd night out with him in Tokyo and Turin. He did make it to the movies, although mostly on the small screen, his main role being one Dennis Phillips, the gay, football-playing boyfriend of ventriloquist Billy Crystal in TV's definitive comedy series, *SOAP*. I don't know if it was deliberate or co-incidental, but Dennis Phillips was the real name of one of America's early 16ft pole-vaulters. Is there anything in this?

A final word on Seagren; he did something in the '72 Munich final that I don't think anyone else in history could have done, except perhaps John Pennel, who wasn't there. Some vaulters, Bob and myself included, had their new '5.50 PLUS' poles confiscated by the German officials before the event, actually it was the night before the event. They in their wisdom had decided that the new, green- coloured pole that we had been using all season provided us with an unfair advantage over those smaller nations who couldn't get their hands on them. It was argued, spuriously, that the East Europeans (Nordwig) and Russians did not have access to them and so were at a disadvantage. What nonsense! If I was able to get one, then anyone who wanted one could. In any case, it was well known that old Wolfgang had tried the '5.50' and didn't like its action, preferring the slower recoil of his black 'Cata-pole'.

Anyway, Seagren was given an untried and untested 'legal' black 'Cata-pole' to use and proceeded to vault to the silver medal. Who won? Guess… Nordwig won gold with a new Olympic record of, wait for it, 5.50m. Is that ironic or not? I don't know how Bob did it but I know for sure he would have won his second Olympic title with his own pole. It's a bit like Schumacher being given an old garage Ferrari to race at Imola and almost winning; or Frankie Dettori placing in the Derby on some old nag. It's impossible.

I will keep a final twist in all this scullduggery for later.

ETERNAL QUEST

Back in Belfast, my frustration at being unable to put into practice all these new ideas was matched only by a determination to solve the problem. The press campaign was resumed in the quest for a suitable hall and I thought I had hit the jackpot when Lady Blackwood generously offered a shed at her riding establishment. The cost of adapting it for vaulting, however, was prohibitive at £200 and no sponsor was forthcoming. It was beyond belief. I know this was early days in the development of sponsorship in sport, but I was the National champion, an Olympic finalist ranked 12th best in the world at the age of 21; and no backer to the tune of £200 could be found. Lynn Davies had a similarly fruitless search for a sponsor for a 'Tartan' rubber runway strip at his Cardiff base… and he was the Olympic Champion. Spartan days indeed!

Eventually I found a spot in a badminton hall through the benevolence of the Ulster Racquets Club and, while it enabled me to get in a few valuable sessions in that post-Olympic winter, the hall was unheated and so cold that frequently the pole wouldn't bend in the severe temperature. So again, on pure fitness alone, I went to the AAA Indoor Championships at Cosford and broke the British indoor record with a good 16ft 3in (4.96m). This spurred the Athletics Board to temporarily put me out of my misery and send me off to the States to compete in its formidable indoor circuit. My immediate host was to be the University of Maryland and its vaulting coach, the inimitable George Butler.

THE KNIGHTS OF COLUMBUS

George Butler was one of those rarities in the US, a top-class specialist technical coach, with a Bob Newhart sense of humour. He would come into my stiflingly hot room in his centrally heated home and, noting that as usual I had all the windows open for fresh air despite the zero temperature outside, he would pop his woolly-hatted head round the door and joke, "Say Mike, what time is the downhill? Those fellas in London, England, didn't tell me you're goin' for the Winter Olympics."

At Maryland University with coach George Butler 1969

During those three winter weeks in the States, under the direction of George, I really consolidated my reputation as one of the leading vaulters. My first meet was at the famous Madison Square Garden in New York and, though I really wanted to do well in front of the appreciative spectators in such an historic venue, I felt tired and jet-lagged and didn't cut any ice. By the time of the second meet, however, I was ready and it was to provide one of my best ever competitive performances. The venue was, fortuitously, in the home- town of my big sister, Kathleen.

The Cleveland Knights of Columbus meet had all the major players present, Seagren, Pennel and all the other American stars. Also present was the McMillan family, in the form of sister Kathleen and her husband Pat, and all their friends, with a big banner bearing the legend '*COME*

ON BELFAST' of which I'm sure the significance was lost on most of the audience but pleased Pat who hadn't even lost his Belfast accent in the twenty years he'd been away. I did not let them down, vaulting a UK and Commonwealth record of 16ft 6in (5.05m) to tie the same height as the USA's own Olympic Champion, Seagren. An official report commented,

> Mike Bull (Great Britain) who recently cleared 16ft 6in in Cleveland, Ohio, a new UK indoor best performance. This was the same height as Bob Seagren who won the competition and is undoubtedly the greatest achievement by a British vaulter.
>
> - The Athletics Coach, March, 1969.

BEWARE GREEKS BARING ALL

The 1969 European Championships in Athens were the focal point of the post-Olympic sporting year and were second only in terms of athletics prestige to the Olympic Games. Largely due to the ongoing problems with my training facilities, this was the first year since I started vaulting that I had not improved on my personal best and so I went into the championships with a 16ft 6in season's best. However, I did have psychologically important victories over Schiprowski and other top Europeans, which included taking the bronze medal in the Turin World Student meet behind Seagren's gold and Dionisi's silver (that darn Italian again). I was also in the best physical condition of my life, again due to the fact that because I couldn't vault in training I had worked furiously on sprinting and strength. My 100m time was now down to 10.7sec, my 400m improved to 48.9sec and I long-jumped 24ft (7.30m).

The climate in Athens was like California, times ten! I loved sun and heat but even I drew the line at 40°C. The GB team captain also loved the sun, so the third part of his motto, 'Bigger, Better and Browner, every day', was not going to be a problem for the reigning European long-jump champion, Lynn Davies. The problem, however, was going to be very real for the majority of the British fair-skinned palefaces, some of whom would be expected to run 5000m, 10000m, and the 26 mile plus marathon in the searing heat. Even Clive Longe, our Guyana born decathlete who took great pride in his very muscular, very black, body had to take precautions!

Some diligent British team official had put temptation in harm's way by arranging accommodation for the whitest team on earth in a beach-side hotel on the outskirts of the city (was he thinking this could be just like Bognar?). You literally opened the patio doors of the dining room and stepped out on to the sand, which of course, many of the 'white-eyes' did on the very first day. The ensuing line of lobsters at the team doctor's room, looking for camomile lotion to soothe the performance-detracting outbreak of sunburn, prompted an immediate team meeting.

The leader of our delegation, Arthur Gold, and our good doctor pointed out the athletic hazards of red-headed, white-skinned Englanders sunbathing in temperatures of 40°C! Arthur called upon our inspirational captain to say a few words on the subject. Lynn, sporting a bronzed visage of which Hollywood actor George Hamilton, old Mahogany Man himself, would have been envious, had just come into the hotel with yours truly after a morning's jogging and stretching and, dare I say it, sunbathing on the beach. He began, "If you are not used to this kind of sun, be careful. If you think it will detract from your performance by one percent, stay out of it. Personally speaking, I like it. It makes me feel faster and jump better. It may be different for you."

It was a perfectly sensible comment really, but the problem was that every athlete in that room wanted to be a European champion, just like the team captain, and they also wanted a tan like his as well. Poor Arthur eventually recovered his composure, but he never forgot the one percent speech. As for myself, the Championships further enhanced my world standing when I only just missed the bronze medal, finishing with the fourth highest vault in a final won by... Nordwig, naturally. Once again, I had relished the excellent training facilities at a major venue, all the time in the knowledge that I faced another winter at home fighting that old David and Goliath battle with a system that simply didn't give a damn about facilities for specialist athletics.

IN WITH THE ARMY

'The Troubles', in fact, led to a temporary solution when the Major in charge of the Paratroop outfit that had taken up residence in Belfast's main exhibition centre made me an offer. In return for my coaching his interested squaddies, I could jump in the main building of the Balmoral Hall with unlimited access. I transported my inflatable pit and the length of broken rubber conveyer-belting, procured from a local quarry, that was used as a run-way – I had discovered the efficiency of conveyer belting back in '68 when I had put it down on top of the old cinder runway at Paisley Park and it had helped me to that landmark 16ft 2½in UK and Commonwealth record. On top of the Hall's wooden floor boards the rubber belting proved a devastatingly fast and springy run-up. The only drawback was that the area for the vault set-up was right in the middle of the soldiers' living area, so, my 140ft of a runway ran right down the line of bunk beds. The fear was the pounding of my spiked feet on the floor as I sprinted down the runway would disturb the paras in their beds, sleeping after another all-night patrol on the dangerous streets of Belfast.

The deal struck to mitigate this annoyance was that I train any of the lads interested in the sport. Corporal Joe Lee was one of the interested volunteers. A 40 year- old career veteran of Aden, Cyprus and Kenya, Joe, with his tattoos and bushy handlebar moustache, cut an unorthodox figure on the pole-vault runway. I loaned Joe an old prototype fibre-glass pole with which to practice, knowing that it was so stiff and un-flexible as to be indestructible. The result was explosive.

Joe was a talismanic figure in the regiment, tough as an old leather boot. He was determined to bend the unbendable and stood at the end of the run-up, gritted his teeth under the 'tache, and charged. The pole did indeed bend, but it also broke and shattered into a hundred pieces with a characteristically loud bang that had all the snoozing squaddies reaching for their rifles as Cpl. Lee somersaulted backwards out of control into the pit, landing in a crumpled heap. He picked himself up and, with a huge grin all over that great face, took a bow to the roar of the cheering soldiers. I definitely want Joe on my side in any world war!

Meanwhile, back in the real world, there were two important things to take care of; firstly, I had to get back to the Philosophy Department at Queen's to complete my Honours Degree and, secondly – what was it – oh yes, Chris and I got married on the 13th of October, 1969.

14. FAMILY MATTERS

It was September 1963, a week before my seventeenth birthday, and we had just started the autumn term back at school. My school pal, Danny, was having a sleep-over (although in those days it wasn't called that) at our house in Sunninghill Drive, but we had plans that did not involve much sleep. In my tiny bedroom we lay in adjoining twin beds, patiently awaiting the signal to make our move, that signal being the deep rumbling tones of my father's snoring in the next bedroom.

Tiptoeing down the pitch black corridor, I motioned to my accomplice to duck under the heavy punchbag hanging from a hook in the attic ceiling trapdoor,

"It'll creak like feck if you touch it!" I had explained to him earlier. Easing open the door of my unconscious parents' bedroom , I reached for Dad's car keys which I knew lay on the nearby dresser, and stealthily backed away with my booty, closing their door silently behind me. We continued down the dark corridor to my sister Kathleen's empty room, empty because she had gone to work as a nanny in upstate New York some years before. Creeping into her room we crawled out of the only tiny window onto the two foot wide ledge which lay a short jump below. Then there was the fifteen foot leap into the dark which would take us safely over the flower bed onto the soggy lawn of the back garden. I was good at this part, the gift of a budding pole vaulter.

My father's car, a bright new yellow Ford Anglia, the one with the distinctive backward sloping rear window, was parked in the street outside our house, within earshot, so much too close to simply fire up the ignition. So we unlocked her and silently pushed the car fifty yards down the street, from where I accelerated away as Danny fixed my L-plates to the windows, because yes, I was a sixteen year old learner driver while my pal, who was seventeen, had a full licence and had been teaching me to drive over the previous few months.

Our immediate destination was the home of a third member of our school version of the Bullington Club, the home and adjoining fish and chip shop of Joe Clerkin's parents. Joe had done the same trick as us and was already sitting in his Dad's big Zypher and, really well organised as usual, had the car packed with a few more school pals and ...wait for it ...GIRLS! (At this point I emphasise to my grandchildren not to try this under any circumstances!)

CHRIS

Our final destination was Danny's parents' caravan. One of the girls in Joe's car was the best friend of his steady girlfriend, Evelyn, who was a very attractive and sophisticated blonde. The friend was something else again, a Julie Christie look-alike with tumbling blonde hair, mini-skirt and white leather boots, but it was her eyes that got my attention, a translucent blue that lit up that caravan. Her name was Chris. Christina Wilson, a student at Oranges Secretarial Academy, was ostensibly there as Danny's date but as the night went on I seemed to be getting on with her much better than him. Chris said she had seen me a few times coming and going at my mother's hair dressing salon in North Belfast's White City- Chris and Evelyn lived nearby, just off the Whitewell Road, and were regulars at my Mum's salon. She knew I was a budding sportsman setting records in athletics while at school, and, alarmingly, said her father followed my fledgling career by cutting out all the local press reports of my exploits. Danny, film star looks notwithstanding (well, he was Junior Mr Ireland!), didn't stand a chance after that. The girl with those blue eyes and this bashful sixteen year-old athlete were mutually hooked!

It never fails to impress me just how much historical perspective compresses events. The next twelve months were truly momentous in the lives of all the players here. Danny got his scholarship to Queens University to read philosophy, Joe went down to Trinity College Dublin to do law (and ended up a founding director of the early Ryanair), Chris graduated from Oranges with world class performances in typing and short-hand and secured a good job in a leading accountancy firm in University Street, and I went off to university on a sports scholarship in the USA. I also passed my driving test, so needless to say that the trips to my mum's salon became more frequent, close by chance, as I said above, to the Whitewell Road?

October 1969 – Our wedding day with Chris looking amazing in her mini-skirt and me in my Olympic uniform, the only suit I had!

My sports scholarship to Southern Illinois University meant being away from home from late August 1964 to June 65, returning home for the summer athletics season and then back to Illinois for my sophomore year in September. The scholarship was for four years of this, but as far as we were concerned, Chris and I were in it for the long haul. The evening before my departure to America we announced to the Belfast Telegraph journalist and photographer, who had come to Sunninghill Drive to cover the story, that we were engaged......much to the surprise of my parents! The next day, there it was in black and white photo and print in the newspaper, Mike packs his suitcase for America, his mother Anne on the left and fiancé Chris on his right, helping him pack. I was 17 years young!

That's more or less what did happen, actually it was 'less' because I transferred from Illinois to Queens in January 1966 when the GB

Athletics team began to rely on my services for international matches and, like Don Corleone, 'made me an offer I couldn't refuse'. The upside of my shock return from the USA also extended to my love life as Chris and I were able to make plans for a permanent future together. We managed to legitimise our 'engagement' when I returned from the 1968 Mexico Olympics with a ring forged from Aztec gold and inlaid with a precious, translucent-blue stone (so the Mexican sales lady had told me). Officially engaged now!

At this point I had graduated with a psychology degree from Queens but had lost my irreplaceable training base in the Shipyard. I had post-graduate offers from Oxford University, Loughborough University, the University of Maryland with coach George Butler, the Royal Naval Academy and from Queens where I was invited to study for a PhD. in Philosophy. The latter came with a hefty (in those days) annual grant of £300; and the promise of a new Physical Education Centre on the banks of the River Lagan, complete with gyms and a purpose-built pole vaulting area indoors in the main hall, to be designed by me. Chris threw into this mix the idea that we could rent a flat in University Street, beside the Library where I would no doubt spend most of my time, and opposite her office where she could continue to earn enough money to keep the wolf from the door. Chris's idea won... or, as my supervisor , Prof Alan Milne, liked to say "It's at moments like this where logic takes you by the throat."

We married in 1969 and lived blissfully in the little flat near the university for a whole year, Chris supplying the bread and me eating most of it! It's nice to reflect that the bread and everything else was sliced with the specially engraved silver cutlery set presented to us by the British Athletics Team as a wedding present. I was also made captain of the team for the coming international meeting. However, just missing out on a medal at the Athens Europeans outdoors and indoors at Vienna was trumped by my big gold at the Edinburgh Commonwealth Games. This significantly raised my stock value and it also raised my aspirations for the next Olympics in Munich. We decided that America was the only route to success. In September 1970 we left Belfast for the lure of Coach Butler's Maryland University, Chris to work as a secretary and me as a research student. The athletics and the coach were great, but it was never going to work. Chris had to work as nanny to a very young and very voluble family of American kids, and I had trouble getting paid employment at the university. Back to Belfast, as my mother said "the shortest emigration in history!"

The next move was even more interesting. My plight for training facilities and coaching was well known in athletics circles and so the top club in the country, Wolverhampton and Bilston, offered me a teaching post and unlimited access to the RAF Cosford arena, the only international indoor facility in the country. Sounded good, a steady income, a secretarial post for wife, a world class indoor training base. I jumped at it.

Cosford on the day of a big championship or international competition was a truly inspirational venue. Thousands of enthusiastic spectators had cheered me on while breaking the UK record on ten occasions, all watched by the sporting public live on TV. I loved it.

Cosford on a cold, dark winter evening, after a day's teaching sociology and sport at Willenhall Comprehensive, was soul-destroying. Alone in this cavernous hangar, I would switch the lights on and stare at the pole vault area and dream of the baying crowd, the TV cameras, the flowing adrenaline on the end of the raised runway. But even a dreamer with an inflated imagination like me couldn't pull it off. I would go through the motions of warming up and jumping but I never had a good session in that deserted shrine. I hated it.

A recurring theme in my story is that just when things hit an all-time low, along comes redemption. In two parts actually; Chris announced that we were expecting a baby, her more than me you understand, but we danced triumphantly. At the same time I was awarded a Churchill Fellowship in Sport to live and train at the fabled University of California Los Angeles, the Mecca of world athletics and home to the world's best vaulters and coaches. Chris went home to Belfast to prepare for the arrival of baby Gavin, due in November 1971. I went to UCLA to prepare for the coming Olympic Games.

Gavin spent his first six months in our tiny flat above a dentist's on the Cavehill Road, close by my parents' home – an important detail in child-rearing. It was here that I invented the night nursing technique of 'remote rocking', where one end of a long rope was tied to Gavin's pram

Family time 1: Posing with Gavin in the garden

outside our bedroom door, the other end being in my active, tugging hand on an otherwise totally dormant body, rocking the baby back to sleep. After all, it was pre-Olympic year and an athlete needs his sleep, my mantra only partially accepted by my forgiving wife.

I'd like to say that reasoned planning was put in place to provide our son with a companionable sibling, but that would be perverse. Baby Natalie arrived during a maelstrom of life-changing events in May 1974. Back at Queens working on that doctorate, I was appointed Lecturer in Philosophy at Ulster University in September 1972. I was in full-on training for the Commonwealth Decathlon, scheduled for February 74 in New Zealand, with training partner Mary P and coach Buster. The appointment allowed Chris to choose her dream bungalow in Carnmoney where we were happily ensconced. Happily, that is, until I had to up and leave her and baby Gavin to travel to California in December 73 to train for a month while en route to Christchurch for the Big One in January/February. To be brief, Chris, heavily pregnant, heroically held the fort with the help of my parents, while I did my bit in NZ. I came back with Gold, was promoted to Senior Lecturer in Philosophy of Sport at UU, travelled to Toronto to vault at the Maple Leaf Games, then to Gothenburg for the European Indoors, to Cosford to win my 12th AAA British Championship, then back to Queens to finalise my thesis and endure my viva (an oral, face to face defence in front of examiners), followed by the awarding of the PhD. Somewhere in all this frenzied activity baby Natalie was successfully delivered –I am quite sure of this because I remember the frantic ride to the hospital with Chris about to deliver in the back of our ageing Mini and then me going from the maternity unit to casualty to get a swollen ankle, injured earlier in training, x-rayed. When I limped back to maternity on crutches a couple of hours later the nurse presented me with a smiling baby girl.

Family time 2: Natatie practising her headstands in the garden

Life was complicated but also exciting. With our young family, Chris and I had times of great happiness and deep fulfilment to balance the champagne and celebratory excesses that came with our successes on and off the track. With hindsight perhaps in these champagne moments there were warning signs for the future but at the time they simply didn't register.

15. The 'Big G'

The focal point now was the Commonwealth Games, scheduled for Edinburgh in July 1970. I had lost my Balmoral Hall training base when the Army moved on and I had, once again, to revisit all the familiar old problems about facilities. At this point it was the intervention of an old friend that solved the immediate, problem. Ron Pickering had moved on from coaching to a career as a BBC sports commentator where his love and enthusiasm for athletics were undiminished. He had set up the 'Champions Fund', which was a resource funded by his business acquaintances to help out the needy present and future championship elite. I was a suitable case for treatment and Ron obliged.

The Champions' Fund enabled me to go to Crystal Palace in May 1970, as soon as university exams were over, to train for almost three months uninterrupted for the July Games. My living accommodation was arranged at the hostel on site and I vividly remember that first day I checked in at reception. There was a small boy in the foyer pacing around in the background, looking me up and down. He could not have been more than 15 or 16 and was really quite agitated but he continually averted his gaze when I tried to make eye contact. The receptionist revealed that he was a young pole-vaulter who had been awarded a revolutionary bursary to live and train at the Crystal Palace Sports Centre and that he had been waiting in the foyer for me since breakfast time. His name was Brian Hooper.

HOOPS

Brian, together with another little schoolboy also called Brian, were the first experimental recipients of a scholarship grant scheme which

A young and slender Brian Hooper leaping into the notorious Crystal Palace sacks of foam rubber

allowed them to live and train at the centre and go to school nearby. It was touted as Britain's answer to the US athletic scholarship but, in truth, the two lads were left to their own devices most of the time and the other Brian soon dropped out and disappeared from the sport. The young Hooper, however, was a different kettle of fish, a very determined 15 year- old indeed.

When I eventually got this boy in the foyer to stand still for a moment and look me in the eye to say hello, he gradually, shyly at first, opened up with a whole series of questions;

"What type of pole do you use?" "How long is your run-up?" "How many days a week do you train?" "What do you eat for dinner?" "What time do you go to bed?" and so on. For every 'you' replace 'we', because Brian had decided that he was going to do everything exactly as I did. He even used to practice walking like me. Then the eternal questioning went on and on all day and into the night;

"What time do we get up?" "Do we vault tomorrow?" "Do you do much gymnastics?" I was getting ready for bed, washing and brushing my teeth and still fielding yet more questions from my new found doppelganger, when I noticed that it had suddenly grown quiet; 'Ah, he's gone to bed at last,' thought I, mistakenly, for there the youth was, crumpled up on the floor of my small room in the hostel, fast asleep dreaming dreams he dare not think would come true – dreams of breaking my record, of being the first Briton over 18ft (5.50m), of making the Olympic final, of becoming World Superstars Champion. They all came true for him. For me, the questions resumed in full flow the next morning.

The simple fact is that Ron's Champion's Fund allowed me to train with ferocious intensity with a single objective in mind, the Commonwealth Games. I trained twice a day every day, rarely straying from the confines of the Centre. I vaulted five days a week in mammoth three hour sessions with the two Brians in support, sprinting and hill-runs every day and weights and gymnastics three days a week. Uncharacteristically, I even passed up competitions, concentrating all my efforts on that date in late July. I trained so hard that I actually experienced a downturn in my vaulting, my legs feeling heavy and lifeless on the run-up with a general lack of sharpness. There was no panic, however, as I knew that once I got to the Games Village my training could be tapered down and the sharpness would return with a vengeance.

EDINBURGH

Edinburgh was the first major games in which I was the favourite. I had been the leading Commonwealth vaulter for three years and, despite the progress made by the Canadians and Australians, this was being viewed as a real opportunity for gold for Northern Ireland. The trick, of course, was to seize this opportunity of a lifetime in the lifetime of the opportunity. The ability to win on the day of a major championship takes a special talent. To be the best for one moment in time, a moment that all your athletic peers are also targeting, doesn't make you the 'best ever', the highest, the fastest or whatever, only the 'best' on that day. It is that very ability, however, that has captured the imagination of writers and experts and the public at large. They wonder and speculate on the unique inner qualities necessary for winning a major title. If there is common ground, then I suggest that determination and self-belief will be at its core; what we call 'grit'.

I certainly believed that I could win but I wasn't to know just how tightly drawn that tightrope between success and failure was going to be. All my hard training had created a dilemma. I was faster and stronger than at any time in my career and, during quality jumping sessions in the Scottish rain and cold, I was overpowering my normally trustworthy 16ft x 190 flex pole. It was getting too 'soft', bending too much and recoiling too sluggishly, which in turn keeps the hips too low to reach maximum heights. So, I immediately ordered a new, stronger and stiffer 16ft x 195 flex pole which, with the help of Lillywhite's sports outfitters, was delivered to me at the Village. Unfortunately, there was only time left before the actual competition for one practice session in which to try out the new implement. In that one session I found out that it was very stiff and would require perfect conditions, good wind and good temperature, and plenty of confidence to use effectively and that I could go very high under these conditions using its greater spring combined with a higher hand-hold. Any weaknesses, mental or physical, would be exposed in a major final. Should I risk it? Winners risk all!

The Big Gamble

The day of the pole-vault final was cool and wet but at least there was not much wind. I opened my account tentatively with an easy clearance of 15ft 5in (4.70m) using the old familiar pole. At the next height of 16ft 1in(4.90m) I was warming to the occasion and to the responsive, capacity crowd and, sprinting faster and taking off more strongly, I hit the crossbar on the way up. This is a sure sign that you are overpowering a 'soft' pole. One failure to me. The two Canadians cleared to take the lead.

Shaking with adrenaline and really fired up, I took 'Big Bertha' out of its cardboard tubular container and instantly made the decision to take my second attempt at 16ft 1in with the new pole. It was a high-risk strategy, especially in the poor weather conditions and with one failure already on my card. Many (more cautious) jumpers in that situation would have compromised, made some slight technical adjustments and eased back a little on the familiar pole and, making sure of success at the second attempt ,would thereby have been able to defer the decision whether to change poles or not until the next height.

What you don't want in this situation is to fail on the second attempt, perfectly possible as the timing may be slightly off, especially on new equipment, and be faced with the nervous third and final attempt – anything can happen when a jumper makes his third attempt, tightening up and trying too hard being a frequent result… and failure. The athletic shibboleth of my training partner, universally acknowledged as the best competitor of his era, Lynn Davies, was by this time drilled into my brain, 'Never Compromise.' Winners risk all! I decided to go for it.

Standing at the end of the runway, the bar at 16ft 1in, a height I had cleared a hundred times before, I was nervous as never before, my heart

Leaping for Gold with 'Big Bertha' – winners risk all!
Photo; courtesy of Mark Shearman MBE

pounding underneath that pristine Northern Irish vest, all my senses heightened and attuned to this athletic environment; the breeze is in my face but it is light enough not to matter; a touch more venice turpentine on the hands to make them nice and tacky; move your first step back nine inches because you know you are going to drive in hard at take-off; stay tall, chest up… let's go, s**t or bust!

There was no time to think about technique on the pole, so strong and fast was its reaction after take-off. It literally fired me high into the air, rocketing me clear of the bar by at least 18in to spare. I thought that's how Schiprowski must have felt in Mexico. It felt good. Sixty thousand people roared their approval. I was back in the competition. More than that, I now knew for sure that I could not be beaten that day. I was in full flow, in the 'Zone'.

The next height was to decide the medals. The same result; I shot clear at 16ft 5in (5m) with daylight to spare on the first attempt. All the others failed three times. The 'Big G' was mine. Northern Ireland had its gold medal. But one person hadn't quite finished. I asked for the bar to be set at 16ft 9in (5.10m), which would be a new United Kingdom and Commonwealth record. The same result; I blasted clear with daylight, only this time it was followed by my first outward show of emotion, as I celebrated with a back somersault on the landing bed and, cheered on by the appreciative crowd, skipped and jogged a lap of honour, certainly not a common occurrence at that time. Only the deteriorating weather and the sporadic entrance of the marathon runners into the stadium prevented me from going on to 17ft plus (5.20m) on that day of days when I entered the 'zone' of perfect synchronicity between mind and body.

But for that fateful decision to change poles things could have been so different; from an Express athletics reporter;

Vaulting wonder Mike Bull reached for the sky in the Edinburgh rain yesterday to capture a Commonwealth Games gold medal for Northern Ireland. Bull's masterly performance underlined his superb competitive temperament, for he entered the competition with the exacting knowledge that he would have to break his own British pole-vault record to collect the gold.

Up, up and away he went to gold, stretching his United Kingdom record by one and a quarter inch to 16ft9in. Bull wasn't satisfied, though. The magic barrier of 17ft had yet to be cleared and, with his confidence at peak level, he was ready for a major break-through.

So, nearly six hours after the competition had begun, Bull attempted to soar to new heights... just as the marathon men entered the Meadowbank Stadium.

The interruption was too much, even for this master competitor and Bull had to be content with the gold. But a 17ft height will be his soon.

THE AFTERMATH

The 'Big G' changed my status in Britain where I was now invited, all expenses paid for myself and my new wife of six months, Christina, to compete at the AAAs. A country club in Surrey would replace the usual camp-bed in a mate's flat, taxis provided to transport poles instead of bribes to said mate's dad. Some things also changed at home in Northern Ireland, where the gold medal was a passport to eternal folk-hero status. In a scene not witnessed in Belfast since Fess Parker did a 'Davy Crockett' movie public appearance at

Receiving my pole vault gold medal at the 1970 Edinburgh Commonwealth Games

the Grand Central Hotel in Royal Avenue in the fifties, ten thousand delirious supporters deluged Aldergrove Airport in a carnival of banners and ticker-tape, welcoming home their heroes, myself and golden girl Mary Peters. A newspaper report portrays a vivid picture;

> Aldergrove Airport ground to a stand-still yesterday afternoon. But it wasn't fog, snow or ice which brought operations to a halt.
>
> It was a heroes' welcome for Northern Ireland's Commonwealth Games team which arrived home from Edinburgh. The baggage claim area was a solid mass of cheering, banner-waving Ulster people who completely engulfed the team members as they tried to collect their suitcases. Principal targets were, of course, Mary Peters and Mike Bull, our gold medallists, and once they eventually got through the main terminal building they were surrounded by more crowds waiting outside. Traffic in and out of the airport was forced to a snail's pace; the coach to Great Victoria Street station had to crawl through the throng; the roadside outside the airport was lined on both sides with cars which couldn't get into the car park while the park itself took more than an hour to clear. After fighting his way through the mobs of autograph hunters Mike eventually managed to get away to a car with his wife Christina — they hadn't seen each other for two months as Mike had been training at Crystal Palace before the Games. For both Mary and Mike it was something they had grown accustomed to over the previous few days since winning their golds. It was part of the reward for success.

Something that was not part of the reward for success was the provision at home of a half-decent training facility. Every time I drove past that damn yellow crane in the shipyard where my best ever facility had once been situated, I grew more frustrated and more disenchanted. In a move born of anger and frustration I decided that I had to get out of Northern

Ireland to stand any chance of reaching my potential. The vaulting world had moved on and 17ft (5.20m) was now commonplace, whereas I had to settle for an improvement of one and a half inches in two years.

Something drastic had to be done.

16. Back In The USA

It was September 1970 when Chris and I decided to pack up and go to the USA, to The University of Maryland, where George Butler held an open invitation for me ever since my successful trip in 1969. However, like most decisions taken in anger, this was to be a great mistake. George was terrific, taking we two athletics refugees into his home and trying to set things up, but I had great difficulty in getting paid employment at the University where I was to join the graduate school to do my doctorate. Chris hated it; the only work she could get without a work permit was as a domestic servant, something she, as a highly qualified private secretary, was rightly reluctant to consider. We lived with the large Butler family, including small kids and teenagers and, under protest, Chris was being groomed as the perfect Irish nanny. Eventually I cracked and, homeward bound after a spell pumping gas and mopping out toilets in an Ohio garage, I took Chris home, thus ending the briefest emigration in history, eight weeks in all. I was right all along, there are no utopias.

Back home with no training facilities, no job, living with my parents and the next Olympics only eighteen months away, things were getting desperate. Such desperation bent my mind to consider the thought that RAF Cosford, the only international status indoor arena in the country, could be an ideal base for training and so I contacted Mike Farrell of the Midland Counties AAA. Mike put me in touch with Bob Roberts and Charles Taylor, who ran Wolverhampton and Bilston Athletic Club, and they found me a job teaching sociology, geography and games at Willenhall Comprehensive School. So off I went once more, this time to a bedsit in Wolverhampton's Tettenhall Road, which was a walking distance from Aldersley Stadium, the home of Wolverhampton and

Bilston, and a fifteen minute drive from Cosford. Chris stayed at home in Belfast initially but joined me later after securing a secretarial post at GKN Sanky. Sounds perfect, no?

Cosford on a dark, dank Monday evening in January, after teaching all day, was not the bright, busy Saturday afternoon carnival of my record setting competitions. It was dead, soulless, Hades in the Midlands. Sometimes I would be the only person there and, having switched on the floodlights in the giant hangar, that famous runway and pit would look austerely cold and uninviting. My results that winter mirrored the uninspiring training conditions and a period of athletic stagnation set in once again. At this point Tom McNab, National Athletics Coach (and award winning author of definitive running saga *Flanagan's Run*) stepped in and suggested I follow the lead of Lynn Davies the previous year and apply for a Winston Churchill Fellowship. Lynn had gone to California to train in the sun and I had jealously listened to his endless tales of epic exploits and athletic adventures in my favourite land. I became the second sporting Winston Churchill Fellow in 1971, having convinced the chairman of the interviewing panel, naturalist Peter Scott, that I, like his famous father, Scott of the Antarctic, was something of a pioneer-explorer.

PARADISE REGAINED – THE CHURCHILL FELLOWSHIP

I struggled to explain to the US Customs officer at Los Angeles International Airport that the contents of my 16ft long cardboard tubes were not, as he suggested, balancing poles for use in an illegal high-wire act, but at least he seemed more familiar with the Jaguar door panels and engine parts that I was also bringing into his country at the behest of the man who was meeting me at the airport. The man was Dick Bank, the foremost athletics journalist in America and a genuine track and field enthusiast who had offered to put me up for a few days until I found suitable lodgings. Dick, overcome with joy at seeing the safe arrival of the spare parts for his beloved Jaguar, drove us straight to the Westwood track, home of the UCLA Bruins, to watch one of the big meets of the season, the annual contest against local rivals, the University of Southern California.

I squeezed past the bulky frame of one of his friends and took my seat in the crowded stand beside Dick and some other of his pals; "Mike, this here's Raymond and this is Marvin, friends of mine and big track fans. Fellas, this here's Mike Bull, England's, sorry Britain's, champion pole-vaulter and Olympic finalist. Winston Churchill has sent him here to train."

Big Raymond extended a chubby, spade-like hand to shake and, lowering his impenetrable shades to reveal large, bulging eyes, he accusingly intonated in a voice that launched a thousand court cases, "Winston Churchill, eh? I bet your father's John Bull?"

"Actually yes, it is," I replied nervously to roars of approval from the gallery.

Well, what would you have said to Perry Mason, for yes, it was Raymond Burr sitting beside me, totally absorbed in the sporting drama on the Westwood stage that afternoon?

To Perry's, sorry Raymond's, left was his own real-life lawyer, one be-spectacled Marvin Mitchelson, who was an even bigger star than his illustrious companion. Marvin had gone down in legal folklore as the creator of the concept of 'palimony' when he successfully represented actor Lee Marvin's common law wife in a very famous multi-million dollar settlement. What did you expect, this was a Hollywood athletics meet, not Paisley Park?

FRANCOIS

The track meet itself was not as entertaining as the gallery. I did, however, pay particular attention to the vault where UCLA was represented by Francois Tracanelli, the world junior (under 21) record holder, on scholarship from France and an old adversary of mine. He won the event brilliantly at 17ft (5.20m), using a technique that had been modified and smoothed out during his time in the US and a hairstyle that had also been modified from flowing, rebellious tresses to a US Marine crew-cut. Over 6ft tall and possessed of a great loping stride that helped him to own one of the highest hand-holds (gripping the pole at 16ft (4.90m)) in the business, Francois, all Gallic flair and extravagance on the pole, was hailed as one of his country's greatest sports prospects.

He was, however, as inconsistent as he was brilliant and I had beaten him the previous year, 1969, in the GB versus France match and in the Athens European Championships, despite the fact that he had posted heights over 17ft 5in (5.30m). It appeared that California was working for him.

At the end of the competition I approached 'Trac' to say "hi" and, with a big grin on his impossibly handsome face, he replied,

"Mike Bull, the great British athlete! You come to my house tonight, we party." I did, and so did he along with Julie, the Los Angeles beauty he was soon to marry and take back to Paris. During the course of the evening it was arranged for me to stay in the spare room in the apartment at Westwood Village which Trac shared with two other athletes on scholarship. That evening, I also met the University's Assistant Coach, Tom Tellez, a man who was to transform my ideas about vaulting and who was to become world famous a decade later as the coach of Carl Lewis. Tom was responsible for the new 'Trac-man', the consistently good French vaulter, and he certainly filled my waking hours with new concepts, fresh drills, film analysis and technical innovation during the three months of my Fellowship.

The apartment was in turn a sanctuary for athletic excellence, with the residents studying for exams and going to bed early after tough training sessions; it was also a madhouse. One of the guys, I think it was Danny Butts the triple jumper, would always make me coffee in the mornings, laced with Jamaican rum, "Great to work out on, man, rocket fuel."

Francois, on the other hand, was totally teetotal, even eschewing red wine, improbably for a Frenchman, expounding the heresy that he believed it produced toxins which caused muscle cramps. Shame on him.

One really hot, Los Angeles summer evening we had all gone to bed early, completely knackered after the day's jumping and training at the track. There was a hot August wind blowing, except this was May, when a blood-curdling scream from the street outside rent the twilight silence. By the time we got out on to the balcony to investigate the L.A.P.D. were audibly en route, their sirens wailing and red lights flashing, and the whole neighbourhood was awake. "Ah, everything's cool," yawned

Trac-man, "only a domestic stabbing. These Santa Anna winds, they drive people crazy."

I went back to bed and dreamed that one day I would catch a Santa Anna tail wind on the runway and shoot clear at 17ft.

PENNEL'S LAST STAND

It was around this time that I met an old friend, actually John Pennel just seemed like an old friend for, in truth, I didn't know him that well at all. The sun was setting on his historic career, now an ex-world record holder and current Marlborough Man in the famous cigarette ads. Hollywood producers hadn't beat a pathway to his door in the way that European track promoters had in the Sixties and John, having done virtually no vaulting since '69, decided to make a comeback. I think it was the fact that I was there as someone to train with that summer, when all the college athletes had gone home for the holidays, that encouraged him to give it a go. Perhaps I reminded him of his iconic status in Europe, whereas in Los Angeles he would be virtually unknown outside of an athletics track.

Whatever the reason, John would turn up at the Westwood track and help myself and another great American 17-footer, Jon Vaughn, pull the heavy landing beds out of the store and laboriously set up the uprights and crossbar. Tugging at the unwieldy foam-rubber wedges, he would bitterly complain to me that it was the years of hauling pole-vault pits about that had given him 'piles'. We all hated passionately the ritual of taking out the landing beds. The only thing we hated more was putting them away again after the session.

After the warm-up John would go straight to the end of the runway and, gripping the pole much lower than in his prime, sprint down the 'tartan' run-up, feet flying and heels kicking as usual, plant the pole and rock back in the same style that had made him the first human over 16ft 3in, 16ft 6in and 17ft… except that now the crossbar was set at 15ft and it was proving to be beyond his reach. It all looked much the same, like he was attempting 18ft, but of course it wasn't, and he wasn't.

I didn't like to see it. Jon Vaughn and I would always start jumping at 16ft, and here was the greatest-ever making hard work of a foot lower.

I think in his heart of hearts he knew it was all over. I ran his diagonals with him, from one corner of the infield to the other, ten times flat out as always, according to his published training sessions, which I had digested in my youth and knew off-pat. We did gymnastics and weights, sprinted and vaulted, but something was missing - not, however, his sense of humour.

I think it was called 'The English Pub', on Sunset, where we went for a bite and a beer. In one corner of the room I recognized the face of an old movie favourite of mine. It was 'Satch' (comic actor Hunz Hall) from *The Bowery Boys*, a comedy act in the mould of *The Three Stooges*, whom I used to watch at the Capitol and Park cinemas as a boy. John was doing his Irish country yokel accent for my amusement and retelling the story of his pretending to be mad at Lynn Davies for spitting out the window of his new Camaro sports-car the year before (he had slammed on the brakes on a busy highway and jumped out to inspect the paintwork for any sign of spittle and had publicly berated Lynn for disrespecting his wheels- to this day Lynn still thinks John was serious). I pointed out that Satch was in the house, whereupon John jumped up and sprinted across to the old star's table. He came back with an autographed beer mat and proudly presented it to me, declaring,

"Mine for his." I happily accepted the trophy and continued eating. A while later Satch himself came across to our table and said to me, very seriously,

"Well, I'm still waiting for that signature, Mr. Churchill."

I'd been set up!

In boxing there is a saying, 'they never come back', and in the case of John Pennel it was true. I lost touch with him after my Fellowship, and the fellowship of gravity-defiers was forever impoverished when the great man fell to cancer and passed away prematurely in Santa Monica, in September 1993. He was 53, the four times world record holder.

FATHERHOOD

The year of 1971 had been, on the whole, athletically disappointing, the second one in which I had failed to improve my personal best (and UK record). A niggling leg injury and my persistent attempts to apply so many new ideas on vaulting had clipped my wings, although there was consolation in winning my 9th AAA title at the new venue of Crystal Palace – the old White City had finally bitten the dust. On the home front, however, things were looking brighter. Queen's University was about to open its new state of the art sports centre by the banks of the River Lagan. Years before, as an undergraduate, I had helped Physical Education Director, Alistair McDonald, plan a sunken box for vaulting in the main hall, with a modern landing bed permanently in place. Could it be possible that 'David' was turning the tide against the old enemy 'Goliath'?

I secured a research bursary from Queen's and went back to University as a full-time postgraduate student to complete my PhD, under the supervision of Alan Milne again. Buster McShane asked me to join Mary Peters and himself in joint preparation for the Munich Olympics, now only ten months away. Chris was back at her old job as a private secretary near the University and we moved into a little flat just round the corner from Mary's.

Oh yes, I almost forgot, Chris gave birth to a bouncing baby boy, Gavin, in November 1971. I wasn't at the track all the time, you know!

17. ONE YEAR, IN SEPTEMBER

Olympia is a sacred place. Anyone who dares to enter it by force of arms commits an offence against the gods. Equally guilty is he who has it in his power to avenge a misdeed and fails to do so.

Ancient Olympic Truce.

THE GAMES OF PEACE AND JOY – MUNICH, 1972

I am not especially sharp at 8 o'clock in the morning but even I, on the morning of September 5th, 1972, as I stepped out of the British Team apartment block on the way to breakfast, realized that all was not normal at number 31 Connollystrasse. Village Security, Munich Police and men in suits were swarming all around the concrete block. I glanced up and saw a guy in a balaclava on the first-floor balcony casually pointing a sub-machine gun.

I come from a part of the world where the first, internalized question asked when there is a violent death is, "What religion was he?"

People in Shlomit Nir's country would ask the same question, only the answer there would be Arab or Jew. Shlomit, or Mitti to her friends in Israel's Olympic Team, was a swimmer and, at an age of only 15 or 16, she would talk about her forthcoming races in the Olympic Pool with a child-like sense of awe and expectation. Lynn, Dave Travis and I shared many cups of coffee with the pretty and personable swimmer at the Olympic Village Milk Bar, where, apparently, we must also have been in the company of one Luttif Afif, a.k.a. 'Issa', who worked and played in the bar. Issa, however, had another agenda. He was the leader of the Palestinian Black September terrorist cell and he was planning to unleash hell.

Mitti's Olympic dreams were to be shattered in Munich. No, she was not a fatality of the Black September massacre; the sexual politics of the IOC illuminati ensured that female athletes were billeted well away from the predatory males and that the only 'hanky-panky' in the Games was conducted behind the closed doors in their corridors of power. She was on a plane heading back to Lod Airport, Tel Aviv, within a few days of our last cup of coffee. Also on the plane were her fellow surviving athletes and the ten coffins of her dead team-mates murdered by the terrorists; the eleventh coffin containing the body of David Berger, the weightlifting graduate of the Columbia Law School and son of a wealthy family from Cleveland, was flown home to his family in the United States on a USAF jet sent by President Nixon. Mitti arrived at Lod Airport at 11.45am on September 7th, amid sweltering heat and melting dreams.

THE ROADMAP TO MUNICH

Buster McShane was seriously rich.

His rampart-enclosed mansion, complete with gatehouse at the imposing entrance, was set in 18 acres of trees and lawn over- looking its own private beach and dock on Belfast Lough just a few miles from Bangor. Inside, it was festooned with wall to wall oil and water colour paintings and crammed with ancient Chinese gongs and vases and displays of valuable antiques. A large Jaguar saloon parked in the pink-pebbled driveway completed the perfect picture of the self-made man.

McShane's name was synonymous with the health and fitness business throughout the British Isles and America. He had made his fortune by being way ahead of the curve in the gym business. At a time when the few gyms that there were, were small 'bar-bell clubs' run on a part time basis, Buster's new purpose built health club in central Belfast's Upper Arthur Street was decorated with hand painted murals depicting heroic figures and events and occupied a prestigious site comprising three floors of the most innovative facilities of any private fitness club in Europe. The reception boasted an excellent health food restaurant and juice bar and a secluded, sunken TV lounge for post work-out relaxation. On the first floor was the ladies' gym with Mary P in charge of all the latest females' fitness barbells and dumb-bells, vibrating slimming belts and tumble-rollers to fight the flab. There was also a full-sized squash court.

The second floor held the men's sanctum, with rows upon rows of loaded bars ranging from 20lbs to 100lbs and dumb-bell sets from 5lbs to 150lbs, squat racks with stacked

Winter of '72 saw regular intensly competitive evening training sessions with Mary P. at Buster's Belfast gym.

loads weighing up to 1000lbs, abdominal boards and wall bars, pulleys and machines for all muscle groups, Olympic bars for the pros, and three or four instructors on hand at all times. In the basement was the piece de resistance, a swimming pool, jacuzzi and sauna. Let me remind you, this was 1972.

Three evenings a week, around 8:30 just as the gym was closing —earlier than the intended 10pm due to the 'Troubles', for Belfast died a death after 8 pm in those dastardly days – I would drive from our little apartment on the Cavehill Road, park in a dodgy side street near the City Hall and explain my way past the Army barriers in Upper Arthur Street. Sometimes my person and my training kit bag would be subject to an exhaustive search, sometimes not. The 18 year-old squaddies manning the steel barriers hadn't a clue who I was and cared less that there was serious business afoot. For if a man like McShane, who had everything most mortals seem to desire, was prepared to spend one and a half hours with me at his gym at the end of a long day's labour in an effort to endow my musculature with the extra explosive power required to propel it beyond 17ft in the air, then to my mind, this was the only serious show in town. For this moment, the bombs and bullets, the assassinations and abductions were all a side show.

Mary P would emerge from a glorified closet where she had been lying prostrate on the floor for twenty minutes relaxation in an effort to recover from the ten hour shift in the gym she had completed – Buster was very good to her but she had to do the hard graft in the gym with an ever increasing membership every day. She was always glad to see me, a training companion at last to share the workload and the dreams of glory. Our strength training programmes were virtually identical and the specified targets similarly daunting, Buster rightly focussing on the explosive power requisite to both the vault and to the five- event pentathlon. I myself would have had a morning run followed by six hours in the queen's University library researching my thesis on 'Relativism'. Chris would have gone to my parents' house for company with baby Gavin at nearby Sunninghill Drive.

When I decided to spend some time in Spain after selling my Bangor home, I came across some of Buster's interminable memos to me on training, all written on the back of brown envelopes. One such exhorted me to try to recapture Peters's 'feeling of excitement, like this is the most important training session in history, for every session.' We had that for a while, we created it together, the three of us, every session was fuelled with a sort of pride, aggression, determination and positivity – I hate that word 'positivity', but that's it, that's exactly what it was. The formula was one very successful businessman/coach, mixed with an extremely single-minded, almost pre-destined for greatness, lady athlete, and stir in a day-dream believer with talent and dedication to burn. That's a very potent alchemy. Some reaction was bound to take place. Base metal to gold?

CITIUS, ALTIUS, FORTIUS

During that off-season training period from late '71 to early '72, I became incredibly strong. My power cleans, an explosive lifting of a barbell from floor to neck height and always a good indicator of athletic strength, improved to 150kg, my bench press to 155kg and Mary and I both half- squatted with a bar on shoulders weighing over 800lbs (365kg). One of Mary's specialist shot-put exercises involved jerking a heavy dumb-bell from shoulder to overhead using her strong, right, throwing arm. She

Vertical jumping, weighed down with a divers lead weight belt to balance the lure of Buster's generous prize fund!

improved to a point where I would have to hoist the weight up on to her shoulder and help lower it back to the floor. It weighed 155lbs (70kg)!

One of my exercises involved strapping lead divers' weights to my ankles and then do 'pop-up' leg lifts overhead while hanging from the wall-bars. Claus Schriprowski would have approved. On other occasions, Buster would place cash on the gym carpet and bet which one of us would vertically jump up to a specified height he had marked out in tape on the side wall of the skylight. This would guarantee a fierce competition between myself and Mary, jumping up into the roof space as if our very lives depended on it, not just the newly minted 50p on the carpet.

It's hard to fully explain, but I felt privileged to be in this company and it transcended mere sport. Here was a man who believed in me. Here was a woman who treated me as an equal. The gym training was special, but it was only the half of it. On the other days we went to the new University Sports Centre where my vaulting sessions took on a new intensity. Mary P would be high-jumping into the same landing bed as me, coming in from the side and, under the close scrutiny of coach McShane, would flop clear at 5ft 9in. The attention then shifted to me,

142ft away at the end of my conveyer belt runway, the pressure really on to make a clear vault at 16ft 5in. Every training session was high quality; every session was a competition. This made the difference, and always will, in any sport in any era.

MADRID AND GRENOBLE

By the turn of the Olympic year I was getting on top of the game. In February I cleared 16ft 7in (5.05m), for a new UK record indoors, to win an international invitation meet in Madrid, beating the new German wonderkid, Ziegler, in the process. In March, Mary, Buster and myself travelled to Grenoble with a small British team for the European Indoor Championships. On the plane, Buster, travelling at his own expense and still very much an outsider to the British Athletics establishment, cracked jokes incessantly and was really good company. I felt proud to be one of his friends.

That weekend I finished fifth highest in Europe with 16ft 5in (5.0m), only prevented from going much higher by a pulled muscle during the warm-up. I had to have a pain-killing injection, which forced me to delay my opening jump until the bar was at the 5m mark, the highest I had ever started and the same as the eventual winner, one Wolfgang Nordwig. At least he now knew I was a contender and showed me respect for the first time by pointing out to me that the bend of my pole was hitting the front landing wedge and stalling my momentum. For Nordwig, The Iceman, this was respect indeed!

THE STOCKHOLM SYNDROME

The outdoor season proved that the hard work was paying off. As Mary P became the nation's third sporting Winston Churchill Fellow (after Lynn and myself) and was packing her bags for California, I went to a rainy and windy Crystal Palace in early June and jumped a new UK record of 16ft 9in (5.11m) to post my first improvement since winning the Commonwealth Games in 1970. Elated, Buster decided that I too needed to get some good weather and competition quickly, so he and a couple of business associates sponsored me, saying,

"Go and see what that Isaacs is doing in Sweden."

Buster's penchant for getting wrong the names of our greatest foreign rivals was really a device to psychologically diminish them, at least in our mind's eye, but it was actually Isaksson, the world record holder at 18ft 2in (5.53m) from Sundbyberg, near Stockholm, that he was referring to. On June 18th I embarked on the trip of a lifetime. I wrote the following in my Sunday Newspaper column of the period;

> At first it's a bit frightening. You have arrived in a strange country. You do not speak the language and you know nobody at all. So, there you are at Stockholm Airport with those 16 foot long poles, wondering maybe you have made a big mistake in coming here. All you have is a phone number. You make the call and the Swedish Athletics Federation seems naturally surprised to hear you, but politely invite you to their office.
>
> Soon your fears begin to fade, everyone is so friendly and helpful, even if you are lumbered with those darn poles. The bus driver, like the passport official, mentions the name 'Isak' as he glances at your strange baggage, and actually seems glad to have you and pole on board – unheard of in Britain.

Isak and Hasse

Then the Swedish hospitality. At the Federation a secretary mothers me like a lost orphan, feeding me with biscuits and coffee, while the director rambles on in his strange tongue on the phone apparently trying to arrange my accommodation. They seem honoured to have me visit their territory and keep repeating, "Eenglish Champion". Imagine Sweden, home of the world's two leading vaulters – Isaksson at 18ft 2in (5.55m) and Hasse Lagerquist at 17ft 8in (5.40m) – being even slightly impressed with little old me. I have met Lagerquist before, so I decide to phone him; he answers "Hello Mike, what are you doing here? Vacation? There's a competition tonight in Eskilstuna. Interested?"

After three hours to Eskilstuna you know every little detail of the rear view of the world record holder, Isaksson, who has been sitting in the front of the car with the charming Lagerquist.

'Little Isak', they call him, 5ft 8in tall but deceptively strong, At first, he seems to me god-like and I shy away from talking to him, not wanting to bore him with my unexpected presence. But I soon realize that he also seems happy to have me on board.

"Good competition tonight Mike. Are you in shape? I may do 18ft (5.50m)."

Well he does not do 18ft. In fact, he makes 17ft and I finish second with 16ft 5in but am close to 17. Suddenly the great Isaksson seems almost vulnerable and I relish the next competition.

THE FIRST 17FT

As I explained in my *Mike Bull's Track Talk* article for the Sunday News June 1972

'Unlike in Britain, the next competition is not far off. In fact, it is the very next evening; and this is their fourth competition in four days. Karlstad is the venue. Five thousand spectators and rain threatening, but good facilities. I feel good, but nervous and start at an easy 15ft 9in, as does one of the newer Swedes, Jernberg. Then the bar goes to 16ft 5in and I have a weak jump but just manage to clear. Jernberg and Lagerquist make it on their third attempts. The bar goes to 17ft ¾in (5.20m) and Isak starts here but fails. So do the other two Swedes. I sense a chance to win. I run hard and think of good technique and suddenly I am sailing some six inches over the bar. I land in the pit. The crowd goes wild. I am not sure if I am dreaming. 17ft. – what I have worked for since Mexico almost 4 years ago. I feel strangely warm as the Press crowd around and take photos and ask about Belfast. Isak fails again. Now he has one attempt left. What a jump! One foot clear and he's in business again. Now at 17ft 6in (5.35m) I have one fairly good attempt, but Isaksson clears easily. After all, he is the world's best. The truth is rammed home to me, 17ft. is just not good enough to win against the best. So on to fresh challenges. Someday, 18ft?'

It is interesting to read this article because it was, quite obviously, my spontaneous reaction to such a landmark in my vaulting ambitions. It is difficult to imagine in these days of astronomical heights just how

Crystal Palace 1972 – Winning my 5th AAA championship and the Olympic trials with a UK record of 17ft 1in (5.21m)

significant the 17-foot barrier was. To me, at that time, it was obviously a dream come true. It always reminds me of the quote from US vaulter, Roland Carter, when questioned after a landmark jump, "My first 18ft vault wasn't any more of a thrill than my first clearance of 15ft or 16ft or 17ft I just had more time to enjoy it on the way down."

THE OLYMPIC TRIALS

Enjoy it I did. The breakthrough was real; a few days later, at Nykoping, I equalled the record height again finishing second to Isaksson. I then went directly from Stockholm to Crystal Palace for the AAA Championships and Olympic trials. The result was another win, my tenth AAA title and twenty-fifth UK National record, this time at 17ft 1in (5.21m) to add one centimetre to the Swedish marks. I was in a purple patch to die for, four UK records in five weeks. Where would it end? James Coote wrote in The Daily Telegraph;

> 'The lessons in pole-vault technique that Michael Bull has received this week from Kjell Isaksson, the athletic Swede who has broken the world record three times in the past two months, has paid dividends sooner than expected.
>
> For Bull, a research graduate of Queen's University Belfast, has after four years of intense effort broken the 17-foot barrier which was becoming steadily more psychological than physical. In leaping 17ft¾in at Karlstad, Sweden, two days ago, Bull finished six inches behind Isaksson but, more important, raised his British record by the handsome margin of 3 and a half inches. Bull is continuing on the Scandinavian circuit for a few more meetings and there is no reason why he should not progress further, especially as he had three good attempts at 17ft 6¾in on Wednesday.'

FINN-ISHED IN HELSINKI

It did come to an end, of course, like all good things. The place was Helsinki, the occasion was the GB v. Finland v. Spain match and the fatal incident was a pre-match warm up session on the evening before the meet. I had jumped poorly in the Helsinki Olympic Stadium the previous year and so I decided to exorcise some demons with a short, sharp vaulting work-out. The wind was unpredictably circling as I took my first run and it caused me to hesitate momentarily before take-off, the worst of all mistakes, and I knew immediately that I was in trouble.

I crashed down short of the landing bed, falling heavily feet first into the box at the front edge in an undignified heap. My ankle bent sideways violently, and I felt a searing stab of pain which made me wretch. Lying there on the ground, I looked at the ankle tightly encased in glove-fitting, suede spikes and saw it balloon into a swollen mess right before my eyes. I was quickly stretchered off, unfortunately in full view of Sandy Gall's roving ITV News cameras and that night suffered the indignity of being a 'bad news' item on the national news flagship. Mike Bull, Britain's Olympic pole- vault hope, stretchered off!

I was one very miserable athlete lying in my hotel bedroom, plastered foot up on a sling, but Lynn and the boys did their best to keep my spirits up with constant visits and many high-jinx. There is some sort of old saying about a good judge of a man being the friends who surround him. I would have been well judged that trip.

Dave Hemery, thoughtful and enigmatic as ever, called in and gave me a copy of an extremely strange little book all about birds which I duly read and eventually, many years later, understood. It was called *Jonathon Livingstone Seagull*, by Richard Bach, which was to become one of those iconic pieces that transcends literature into a sort of cult allegory of the age. Dave's point was, I think, that champion athletes are 'very strange birds indeed.'

Alan Hubbard wrote of the accident;

'Britain's star pole-vaulter, Mike Bull, crashed and injured himself during a training session on the eve of Britain's athletics match against Spain and Finland in Helsinki last night. Bull, 25-year-old Commonwealth Games Champion from Belfast and the first Briton ever to vault 17ft, badly damaged an ankle and may miss the match. Teammates rushed to his aid at the Olympic Stadium when he fell backwards after taking off and crashed into a small wooden pit beside the landing area (sic).

Long jumper Lynn Davies was among those who helped to carry Bull to the dressing room. Davies, who will be Britain's team captain in Munich, told me: "It looks like a very bad sprain. We've no idea yet whether he will be able to compete. It probably needs an x-ray. I have seen Mike get several injuries before, including a broken nose, and carry on. But this is different. He could be incapacitated."

Bull, a university lecturer in philosophy, had arrived earlier with the British team and had only just started to practice jumps at the stadium, where the match will be held. He said; "I actually fell in the landing area but I caught my ankle on the edge of it and slipped down into the box. It is very painful and I have no idea whether I will be able to compete."

However, with Munich approaching, British officials will take no risks with Bull. He was ordered to bed and may miss the match, which would be a big blow not only to British hopes but to the Finnish fans.'

Running Out Of Time

The Munich Games pole-vault was scheduled for September. It was now the 25th of July and I was crocked up with ankle ligament damage with only five weeks to go. Back home in Northern Ireland, there was no system of physiotherapy treatment for athletes. There were other priorities in the days of 'Bloody Friday' when our local shopping area was blown apart by IRA bombs, as was a large area in central Belfast. Patrick Collins wrote in his Munich File;

British athletes, we shall be told, are faint-hearted, under-prepared, overrated, non-triers who have taken that business of competing rather than winning far too literally.

In anticipation of that inevitable chorus, it may be well to point out the unique disadvantages under which British athletes are required to labour. Mike Bull's case will serve as well as any.

Bull is a pole-vaulter, the practitioner of a lonely, hazardous event which makes enormous demands on an athlete's nerve, speed and technical ability. He possesses all three qualities in an abundance which would guarantee him an athletic scholarship in America or an Army commission in Eastern Europe. But we don't do things that way...

In Britain he is required to work out his own way of affording the flexible, fibre-glass poles which cost between £50 and £60 each. He has been forced to tour the country in search of landing pits to guarantee his safety.

Bull has been asked to reach out for world class without the essential stimulus of domestic competition, since nobody is capable of challenging his domination. And, just to ensure that his road to Munich is not unduly smooth, he has conducted his Olympic preparation in a province desperately close to civil war; 'After the things which have happened in Belfast, it's pretty trite to complain about not being able to train properly for an athletics event,' he says. 'But the troubles here haven't done my preparation any good. It was all going pretty well for me at last. I'd had a bad time when I had to move to Wolverhampton and train on my own in a huge great hall which happened to have a proper pit. But then I got the chance to do research at Queen's University, with fabulous vaulting facilities. Then I began to clear 17ft pretty regularly. I felt really good, but the bombings started up again. I have to go right across town to reach the training centre and that means road-blocks and checks and searches. Then we had our shopping centre blown up on that terrible Friday. I'd been there 20 minutes earlier. It really shakes you, that.'

As Bull says, in Ireland's situation, complaints about sport sound trite. But he has worked so hard for Munich that any hindrance is heartbreaking. The fools, of course, will not be stifled. If Bull does not qualify for the Olympic final, he will be counted a failure. Yet it is not, one feels, a word which can be applied to a dedicated man who journeys across Belfast every day of his life to learn how to control a whipping, wayward pole and catapult himself 18ft into the air.

Well, I did make it to the Games. A late fitness test involved me going to Edinburgh for an attempt to prove I could jump, under the scrutiny of the Chief National Coach, John Le Masurier. I had my ankle taped up so tightly I couldn't feel a thing, but I also couldn't run very efficiently. I did manage to get air-born and take off, disguising a fleeting wince and knocking the bar off three times at 15ft 9in (4.80m). What a down-turn in the space of a few weeks! The coach, however, passed me fit. Munich was on, even if my ankle wasn't, but a gammy leg was to be the least of the problems at the Games of 'Peace and Joy.'

SHADOWS IN THE CAVE

Ankie Spitzer deeply loved her husband Andre, the Israeli Team fencing coach who was one of the victims of Black September. Simon Reeve in his brilliant book *One Day in September* (Faber and Faber, 2000) writes of Ankie in terms that also encapsulated my feelings at the time;

> Ankie Spitzer arrived just in time for the service. She was met at the airport and then taken to the Olympic Stadium. There were just a few minutes before the service was due to start, and Ankie had to run through the Village towards the stadium. As she did, she glanced from left to right, and could see athletes limbering up and training for their events. 'I said, "This is surreal!" I'm running through the Olympic village and people are training and I'm running to a memorial service of eleven athletes who were just murdered. How are they still doing sports? I could not understand it.

The history of Munich has been written and documented and Reeve's book is the definitive text. The takeover of the Israeli block by eight heavily armed terrorists from an extreme faction within the Palestinian Liberation Organization; the immediate shooting to death of two athletes in their room; the unceremonious dumping of Moshe Weinberg's body, the side of his face shot away and his chest blown open, in Connolly Strasse; the protracted negotiations and demands for the release of Palestinian prisoners; the deal to fly the terrorists and eleven hostages from Furstenfeld Bruck military airbase; the growing media and sightseeing scramble at Furstenfeld Bruck; the bizarre announcement made by a male spectator or civilian wearing an official Olympic hat, at the perimeter of the airbase, to the effect that "everything is fine! The hostages have been released!"; the collective sigh of relief back at the Village when Reuters dramatically reported to the world, *'All Israeli hostages have been freed.'*; the front-page headlines of the Jerusalem Post, *'Hostages in Munich released - all safe after Germans trap Arabs at Military airport.'* the good news spreading like wildfire throughout the teams in the Village; then the correction within hours by Reuters, *'FLASH! All Israeli Hostages Seized By Arab Gunmen Killed.'*

Jim McKay of ABC News broke the story to the world; "Our worst fears have been realized tonight... They've now said that there were 11 hostages. Two were killed in their rooms yesterday morning. Nine were killed at the airport tonight... They're all gone... It's all over... What will happen to the Games of the XXth Olympiad? None of us knows... What will happen to the course of world history?... I have nothing else to say..."

And that was that. We athletes knew little of what was going on and what was being said. We were like the dwellers of Plato's cave, looking at the wall behind our campfire, where only the shadows of what is going on outside the cave are being cast as representations of reality in the outside world. I thought we were all going home, the Games cancelled. But Avery Brundage, the elderly President of the IOC, announced in his American accent at the memorial service in the Olympic Stadium, to everyone's surprise, that there would be a one day's cessation of the Games as a mark of respect and that they would thereafter resume as normal. Business as usual.

Many athletes felt differently. The entire Philippines' athletics team left Munich. Six members of the Dutch team did the same in protest at the 'obscene' decision to continue. A quarter of the Norwegian team said they would not continue "when 11 of our sports colleagues have been murdered." The two American marathon runners, Kenny Moore who came fourth, and winner Frank Shorter, dedicated their efforts as a personal memorial to the dead Israelis.

We in the British team remained in the Village and tried to pretend that our sports competition was important. I don't remember many details of the vault, beyond the sleazy board-room decision, already outlined in Chapter 8, to confiscate all the new, '5.50 Plus' poles, and the fact that my ankle injury prevented me from running properly on the runway. Of the former, I wrote subsequently;

'POLE VAULT TRAGEDY - where at least six vaulters were asked to qualify at ten in the morning using poles they had never even touched before, because of those crazy, no-yes-no decisions about whether or not they could use the latest American pole. That's like giving a Formula One driver a spare car in qualifying. I am, of course, thinking sympathetically of defeated champion Bob Seagren. But I know one Canadian who was so confused he entered the stadium without any poles of his own at all - he failed to qualify, of course. Thanks to some petty stupidity and ignorance on the part of the Olympic technical committee, the pole-vault was the greatest Olympic non-event ever! If the Games are to survive, the organisers must get back to the fundamentals of the whole thing and give priority to the competing individuals instead of over-doing the flag-waving nonsense.'

Among the six vaulters referred to here, apart from myself, were Seagren, eventual silver medallist, Steve Smith (US 18 footer), Isaksson and that old Italian rival, Dionisi. Only Seagren, silver medal winner, coped with this situation. All the rest of us performed dismally. It still hurts me to think about this but this newspaper article states the bare facts;

'It was an unhappy Bull who walked away from the vaulting pit... Mike, a Queen's University philosophy graduate, entered the competition at 15ft 9in and cleared the bar at his second attempt. But when it went up to the next height of 16ft 5in he failed on all three attempts even though he has cleared 17ft on several occasions this year. Commented a British team official: 'It is fairly obvious Mike has not fully recovered from the injury he received in Finland recently. But that is not an excuse. If he wasn't completely fit he should not have been in Munich.''

DISILLUSIONMENT

There is no doubt that I reacted badly to the Munich experience. With hindsight it would seem likely that coming from war-torn Northern Ireland worked against whatever emotional stability I was trying to maintain. You might have thought it would be an advantage, living day to day on a diet of terrorism and social disruption at home, to be a Northern Irishman thrust into the Munich maelstrom.

But I believe the opposite was true, the surreal perception of armed militants on the roof-tops in the Village was, for many athletes, just that, surreal. For me, it was all too real. Athletics was my personal 'great escape' from an intolerable situation at home. It had enabled me to travel endlessly to the most glamorous and congenial places in the world in this privileged and almost false pursuit of sporting achievement. Sure, like anybody else I had always to go home, but for me there was always the next trip, the next competition, the next major championship to anticipate.

Now, however, that great escape route was being closed down. Not even the Olympic Games was safe. It is also true that I was carrying a debilitating injury, the sort of ligament damage that only rest would cure. All that strength and conditioning with Mary and Coach McShane, all the confidence of those 17ft-plus jumps which had made enthusiasts think of me as a potential medallist, everything quickly went down the plughole. In practice in the Village I could not keep the bar on at 16ft 5in (5.0m), a height that formerly I could have cleared any day of the week. My mood was down and a natural predisposition towards introspection and self-analysis just made things worse.

Journalist Bryn Davies encapsulated this emotionally charged reaction;

> 'A top British athlete last night condemned the Olympic movement and declared he will never watch, let alone compete in the Games again. Pole-vault star Mike Bull disclosed his disillusionment after a season which heralded the breaking of the 17ft barrier by Belfast's British record holder and ended with him depressed and dispirited in the Olympic Village. "My ambition has always been to win an Olympic medal, but now I don't care if I never take part in the Games again. After the torment I suffered in Munich, I don't even want to watch another Olympics," he confessed. Twenty-four-year-old Bull, who revealed his failure at last month's Olympic final was mainly due to an injured ankle which has still not healed, likened the Munich village to 'a concrete jungle.'
>
> "It was overcrowded, and I didn't even know where I was half the time. My temperament, and that of athletes like Ron Hill, isn't suited to that environment. I was disturbed by the militarism and uniformity which shrouded the Games. The nationalism, which surrounded the whole competition, is a great problem. Perhaps I'm being too sentimental. Most athletes are more extroverted. They are completely wrapped up in their events. But for me, the fun has gone out of the Olympics. The impression struck me instantly that there was to be none of the joy of Mexico, and I spent all the evenings in my room, depressed by it all."'

A suitable case for treatment!

18. The 'Big G', Part Deux

One year after the doom and gloom of Munich, athletics writer Peter Hildreth wrote on September 23rd, 1973;

> And paramount in the field events was Belfast's Mike Bull, who scaled a new U.K. national pole vault record-at 17ft 2¾in (5.25 metres). Stimulated by the presence of European record holder Kjell Isaksson, Bull surpassed by four centimetres his own record established in July of last year. Thus, after a season in which he started rather unconvincingly, Bull now looks a strong contender for another medal in next January's Commonwealth Games where he will be defending the title which he won in Edinburgh in 1970.

A Modest Proposal

What a difference a year makes! That result in winning the GB v. Sweden match put me back on top. That and gaining a bronze in the European Cup Final with 5.20m in a wet Commonwealth Stadium in Edinburgh, put me back in contention.

With Mary P's Olympic Gold safely on the mantlepiece, coach McShane succeeded in convincing me of his long-held conviction that I too could be the best all-rounder in the world. I imagine that for him the challenge of taking someone to gold in the ten event decathlon, having done so in the women's five event pentathlon, was irresistible. For me, it seemed a way of rekindling the fire of ambition that Munich had all but extinguished. It was now all about 'project decathlon', winning the Commonwealth Games decathlon in January '74 with a view to the Montreal Olympic event two years later. However, there is that old saying along the lines of, 'create a five-year plan (in our case four year) and make God smile.' It's that old hubris-nemesis game of Grecian roulette.

Things were back on track both athletically and domestically. I secured a Lectureship in Philosophy at the University of Ulster and a 25 year mortgage on a beautiful little detached bungalow in Carnmoney, not far from the college. Mary and I started putting in all the hard training, weightlifting, running, hurdling, jumping and throwing at the gym and at the Queen's University sports centre, with Buster the guiding hand and constant source of encouragement.

THE DECATHLON

Surrounded by some of the equipment required for the decathlon as a teenager
Photo; courtesy of Belfast Telegraph

I must say I liked the variety of training for the different events. McShane would draw the various strands together with observations like, "The key for 'us' is the 100m. 'We' must be good enough to beat everyone around here, regularly running 10.4sec. Otherwise 'we' are just not fast enough to compete with Jennings." He liked to use the 'royal we' and the usual deprecatory misnaming of a rival, referring to the American record breaker in decathlon, Bruce Jenner as Jennings. I was not yet in Jenner's class, but I was getting faster and stronger than ever. My power cleans improved to 160k and bench press to 170k and my bodyweight was packed with additional muscle for throwing the shot and discus. The extra muscle helped my speed – just look at the physiques of modern muscular sprinters – and I was timed at 10.5sec for the first leg of a relay, compared with my official fastest time of 10.7sec.

We worked every day at hurdle drills, aimed at increasing the lateral flexibility of my right hip joint to accommodate sprinting over ten barriers 3ft 6in high. Vaulting had given me good linear flexibility in terms of hip flexion and stride length, but I was quite tight in this new hurdle posture.

My high jumping improved rapidly as I got the hang of the Fosbury Flop technique and I soon beat 6ft 1in (1.85m). The long jump should improve naturally with greater speed and Buster had set a target of 25ft (7.60m), as opposed to my best of 24ft (7.32m).

Long jumping at Queens University [PB 24ft (7.31m)]
Photo; courtesy of Belfast Telegraph

The throws were sound enough, except for the javelin. I couldn't get my throwing arm and shoulder into a position to apply the force of which I was well capable. The years of vaulting had developed a certain rigidity in my right shoulder joint and javelin throwing was always very painful. Eventually, Northern Ireland javelin champion and fellow decathlete, Bill McCarron, came to the rescue. Bill, with typical generosity and great patience, pulled me aside and made me agree to meet him regularly to work on my weakness. He was an excellent coach and a great student of athletics and he succeeded in giving

Discus throw at Queens University [PB 145ft (44m)]
Photo; courtesy of Belfast Telegraph

me a viable technique whereby I could throw without hurting my shoulder every time. I learned to cope but I never mastered the event and later, it was almost to be my undoing in the Games – weaknesses will always be exposed in major championship finals.

As for the dreaded 1500m, the decathlete's nightmare, it would, in most cases, be a function of the general fitness of the athlete. Although Tom McNab, British National Coach for multi-events at the time, said I had a real flair for the metric mile after running a 4min 30sec in a match against France, there was never much time spent on this lean runner's event. The cost-benefit equation never works out in what is a power-biased event; no sense using up energy for so few points .

END OF A LEGEND

The plan was on course. After one particularly tough evening in the gym, Buster invited Mary and I to his Belfast Arts Club for a drink, orange juice in our case, with his greatest friend, ex-Irish rugby international, Deryk Monteith.

The jokes were really flying, and the company was good, Deryk and Buster swopping anecdotes and insults amid raucous laughter, just as they had earlier been doing on the squash court. Nevertheless, at around 11pm, the two dog-tired athletes took their leave and headed home, Mary and me of course. The other two 'athletes' happily stayed on.

I am always wary of the pre-breakfast doorbell ring and, on this cool April morning in 1973, that wariness was justifiable. The policeman at the door informed me that coach McShane had been involved in a fatal car accident. In one instant, the life force that had always seemed indestructible had been snuffed out. At first, I was angry. How could the fates conspire to do this to me? With typical athlete's selfishness, I was asking myself how I could be expected to take on alone the world's best decathletes. I saw Christchurch and Montreal slipping away. This was quickly overtaken by genuine sadness. The world of sport was a poorer place without the mercurial little dynamo. There was certainly much less raucous laughter. Mary P was quite simply devastated. I didn't think she would ever get over it. In many ways she never did. But at the funeral and cremation in the little church at Roselawn on the outskirts of Belfast, one of Buster's old pals and former Mr Britain, Billy Cooke, spoke of the future;

"You and P have to go on. The wee man wanted you both to win gold in Christchurch". Cookie, a self-made millionaire from Belfast, lived in Bermuda and subsequently sent us two air tickets to join him in that sunny island for a holiday and to get 'the head right.' Mary was able to go but my teaching job did not permit. Our decisions were taken independently.

THE DECISION

We decided to go on with the project and to dedicate the effort to Buster's memory. Training resumed and soon too did competition. Competition for me had always meant vaulting and I had no clear picture of an alternative, there being only a couple of decathlons a year. Unlike my celebrated successor, Daley Thompson, the greatest decathlete of all time, I really did not have a structured plan to utilize big meetings and championships as a means of improving all ten events. I was used to entering and winning, at least on the domestic front, one event only, the pole-vault. As a result, I was caught between a rock and the proverbial hard place.

Living in Northern Ireland and not being a known decathlete, I was not going to get an invitation to Crystal Palace or Rome to long jump or throw the shot. I was still doing all round training and a variety of events for my Wolverhampton club, but my vaulting was suffering. I was still UK number one, although that young Brian Hooper was fast catching up on me. Gradually my vaulting got back on song, helped by selection for international duty in Innsbruck, Leipzig, Athens, Oslo, Stockholm, Karlstad, Moscow, Crystal Palace and Edinburgh. This last was the venue for another one of my best ever performances, third place in the European Cup Final with 17ft¾in (5.20m), on a par with that 1970 Commonwealth Games win.

Squeezed in between all this was one encouraging multi-event performance at the Scottish Decathlon Championships at Meadowbank where I put together a reasonable series of results to break through 7000 points for the first time with 7107 points. On the strength of this I was made captain of Britain's multi-event team to meet France in an international fixture to be held at Crystal Palace. I finished third, the top Briton, in the decathlon match which incorporated the AAA Decathlon Championships but, despite being the top Brit, I was not credited with winning the AAAs. They said they lost my application form! It would have taken my AAAs titles record to 14 and kept my name in the Guinness Book of Records a little longer.

The '73 season ended with that vault victory against Sweden and the 17ft 3in British record. I was now being viewed as a candidate for gold in both the vault and decathlon at the New Zealand Games, scheduled for January '74. Encouraged, I continued to train for both events, with Mary as always, but the single biggest problem facing all of us in the Northern Hemisphere was the seasonal anomaly of a major games in the depths of winter. It was, of course, mid-summer in Christchurch. How do we get into peak competitive condition for this one?

CALIFORNIA AGAIN, PEARLS OF WISDOM

Cathy Pearl ushered us into the lounge of her rambling down-town Pasadena bungalow, from where loud organ music was emanating. Inside, the drapes were closed to the bright Californian sunshine outside, and in the gloom the barely recognizable shape of Bill Pearl, seated in front of a piano-organ, was in full flow of a rousing musical score. His wife shouted over, and Bill stood up to greet us. The music continued playing without missing either a beat or its maestro, for it was a preprogrammed organ music machine! Talk about the phantom of the opera!

I know, I have said it before, but what do you expect? This is La-La Land. Mary and I had decided to go to California in December for sun and inspiration. Dick McColgan, the perennial force behind Northern Ireland's Commonwealth Games efforts, got the necessary funds to send us, and my employers at college were supportive. We stayed with John Forde, an old friend of Buster and former physique champion from Belfast. Once installed, we decided to look up one of Buster's great friends who just happened to own one of the best gyms on the coast, in which we planned to train during our stay.

Bill Pearl was the Arnold Shwarzenegger of that era. He was the youngest, at age 20, to win the Mr. Universe and then at 40, the oldest. An eccentric is, by definition, someone whose behaviour is abnormal, someone who refuses to conform to the accepted conventions of his society. To say that Bill was eccentric was something of an understatement. I immediately liked him when he said that it would soon be time to work out. My affection mellowed somewhat when I realized that he meant by 'soon' the ungodly hour of 5:30am, his normal training time, and that since it was now past 9pm it was time 'to turn-in. '

Bill arguably knew more about strength training than anyone on the planet – his later book 'The Keys to the Inner Universe' is a timeless classic – but some of his ideas were a little off-beat. After our workout in his superb gym, I was looking forward to a dip in the Jacuzzi to ease my aching limbs but was a little put off by the sight of the Mr. Universe entering the shower area wearing a raincoat. He got into the cubicle, hung the coat up, showered and put the coat back on again for the short walk to his office to dress. He explained, "I'm a pro. No-one gets to look at the bod for free!"

At the time, Bill had reduced his bodyweight from 260lbs to 185lbs by diet and daily cycle spins of 40 miles through the Valley. He explained he was on a life extension programme. He insisted, however, on wearing the same short-sleeved shirts, the arms of which were now down past his elbows of his new, comparatively slight frame. He had also become a vegetarian and, like everything in his life, there was no middle ground.

Mary and I were invited to Christmas dinner at the Pearl's maternal home and his mum made a lovely traditional turkey spread. Bill played with his plate of food, studiously avoiding all turkey while contriving to hide from his mother the alarming change in taste of the boy who used to eat a pound of prime steak for breakfast. During a mutually timed visit to the loo, Bill looked agitated and asked me if I had seen them. "Seen what?" I enquired.

"The maggots in the turkey meat" he replied.

I think those old Santa Anna winds must have been at work again. They make people crazy you know!

BILL CUNNINGHAM AND ERIC DOWEY

Some of Buster's old chums were relatively normal. We looked up Bill Cunningham, a former Irish physique champion originally from Belfast's Shankhill Road. Bill had worked as an instructor in the famous Vince Gironda Gym in Los Angeles, where many Hollywood film stars

With Eric and Lynn on holiday in Spain

passed through his expert hands. One such owed much of his coming success to the Belfast man's training methods when he was put through his paces in the gym to gain some solid muscle for a forthcoming role. The actor was Charlton Heston and the role was Ben Hur.

On trips home in the 90s, Bill Cunningham, who had by then become owner of his own Fitness Instructors Academy in Los Angeles, visited me at my Bangor Gym for a workout and for an update on life in California. Close to 70 years of age at the time, he had been the over-60 Natural Mr. California, and had possibly the best physique I have ever seen for a man of his age. The only possible exception was Bill's great friend and mentor, Bangor's own Eric Dowey, who instructed for me and trained with me at my gym for 25 years and who won the Natural Mr. Britain and Mr. Olympia at the same age-group ('Natural' means drug-free in these contests). Eric (now in his 80s) and Bill still train every day and will continue to do so, D.V., for a long time to come.

THE OTHER MARY

We left California prematurely due to what they call a storm, in fact a belt of rain which offers nothing but unsettled weather for a couple of weeks. Before we left for an earlier than planned exit to the antipodes, Mary P contacted an old sister campaigner in the British team, Mary Rand, the former 'golden girl' (the original) of World Athletics who won gold in the long jump, silver in the pentathlon and bronze in the relay at the Tokyo Olympics, and who was now Mary Toomey. She could have had the choice of a wide field of admirers (including yours truly) but had fallen for and married the American winner of the Mexico Olympic decathlon, Bill Toomey.

Bill was at this time coach to the University of California at Irvine and he arranged for us to train at the college track. Mary was the glamorous housewife, looking every inch the perfect physical specimen she undoubtedly was. I had difficulty coming to terms with the golden girl ironing the t-shirts of any man, albeit the greatest all-round male athlete on the planet. So too did she; "Godamnit Bill, what's the point of me smoothing these effing shirts when you're just goin' straight out to roll in the grass in them?" Bill, horizontal on the sofa, recuperating you understand, grunted sympathetically. Mary, not impressed, "Look at him. The greatest athlete in the world. The laziest!"

As we drove away from Irvine two images were foremost in my mind. First, the frustrated expression on the face of Casey Carrigan, the new American number one vaulter, who in out-of-season shape had to give second best to my consistent 17ft jumping in training. Second, the two gleaming 'His and Hers' Mercedes Benz sports cars parked by the track in the spaces marked 'TOOMEY'. I suppose ironing T-shirts had some compensation.

THE LAND DOWN UNDER MEETS ' JENKS'

We were almost the first athletes to arrive at the Commonwealth Games Village in Christchurch in early January 1974 but David Jenkins was there before us. 'Jenks' was my new buddy and team-mate in the British team, since the retirement of Lynn Davies after Munich. We shared a passion for the sport and for life, the music of Eric Clapton and J.J. Kale and good food, being uppermost. If you thought that Bill Pearl fitted the proffered definition of 'eccentricity' then you ain't seen nothin' yet; Dave was different!

He was also rather good at running the 400m flat out. European Champion at the age of 19, Dave was the first non-American to win the American national championships in an event in which eight out of the top ten in the world were Americans. His winning time was 44.9sec and would probably still make most Olympic finals. His early coach, John Anderson, the man who finally found fame by bellowing "Are you ready?" in the popular *Gladiators* TV programme, introduced Jenks to me at Crystal Palace and admitted that he found it 'interesting' that his young protégé had adopted laid-back old me as a travelling companion in the gladiatorial arenas of the world.

And travelling companions we were. In our Athens hotel room one morning at dawn, I was awakened by a commotion outside in the corridor. I staggered bleary-eyed to the door and witnessed a first; Dave was practicing sprint starts out of blocks in the hotel corridor… b**lock naked!

I grew accustomed to such eccentricity. I introduced him to a girl he fancied, my wife Chris's best friend, Evelyn, a very attractive blonde from Belfast. One morning at his house in Gateshead he announced to one and all that he thought Evelyn had cancer, because she smoked, and he barely spoke two words to her for the rest of the trip. I tried to explain to her that strangeness was the price of genius. It didn't work. Evelyn dumped him!

One morning at 8 am sharp in our hotel room in Poland, I think (or it could have been Athens), the phone rang to announce to its sleeping occupants, Jenks, Brian Hooper and myself, that the team bus was about to leave for the air-port and would we please get on it immediately. My heart kicked into second gear as the adrenalin coursed through alcohol-laden veins but, as I pulled the duvet off Hoops's bed and screamed for urgency, I was amazed to see Dave wake up, pack, dress and close the door behind him in the time it took Hoops to put feet to the floor!

I stayed one summer with him in a flat in Highgate he shared with Welsh Commonwealth Games hurdles champion, Berwyn Price. Breakfast was early because Dave didn't sleep much, on the grounds that he wasn't in the business of staying still. You could rest assured that, following a breakfast of half-dozen scrambled eggs, ten rashers of bacon, beans, tomatoes and mushrooms, there wasn't much stillness.

Dave (aka "Jenks") the reigning European 400m Champion, was a great comrade at arms, a highly intelligent Scottish Public schoolboy and graduate in chemical engineering from Edinburgh University. He was a highly motivated athlete, the first Briton, along with Alan Pascoe and Brendan Foster to put the case to the establishment that there should be a new international ethic in the sport, 'no dough, no show'. It was probably that drive and restlessness which got him into trouble eventually, when he served time in a California State Penitentiary for drug trafficking offences. At the time, I tried, but couldn't reach him. He did his time.

Highly charged, erratic, neurotic, whatever, it was Dave who met Mary and I off the plane in Christchurch and showed us to our quarters, to the restaurant, to the recreation areas and to the training facilities in the Village. They were all magnificent, wide open grass areas for running and throwing and specialist jumping and vaulting facilities. The weather was hot and sunny in a way that was clear and unpolluted and ideally suited to high performance track and field athletics. I was getting that warm, inner glow again. I was in my element and in my prime.

A SUDDEN SCARE

And then it happened. Inexplicably, one morning as I arose in the little room I shared with Northern Ireland's youngest, newest, sub-four-minute mile sensation, Paul Lawther, my back went out of sync. Muscles stabilizing my thoracic spine, between the shoulder blades, spasmed like a knot in a rope and were preventing me from breathing let alone moving. Young Paul bellowed for team manager McColgan, who in turn yelled for an ambulance, which promptly conveyed me to casualty. I was given a muscle relaxant jab to help my breathing and hot stones were applied to my back to try and relax the spasm. I was discharged that evening with the advice to forget about the decathalon.

In some of the largest headlines ever witnessed in the Belfast Telegraph sports pages, the scare story went out;

BULL - DISC TROUBLE SCARE

Anxiety today in the Ulster Games camp. Mike Bull, favourite for another Gold Medal, has been ordered to break training for a couple of days after a back injury scare.

Bull- he is the reigning Commonwealth Games champion in the vault- got a nasty shock when he tried to get out of bed here this morning. He rolled over and dislocated a vertebra in the spine. A doctor was hurriedly called and manipulated the disc back into place. Happily, the injury doesn't seem to be serious. There has been definite improvement in Mike's condition over the past 12 hours.

Bull launches a Gold Medal bid next Saturday in the gruelling 10-event decathlon. WILL HIS BACK STAND UP? That was the 64-dollar question here today.

THE CHRISTCHURCH DECATHLON

Sudden injuries like that have a way of eating into an athlete's self-confidence. Was I being revisited by the demons of Munich? Before the injury things had been going so well in training. Bill Toomey, in Christchurch as a representative for the manufacturers of the track's running surface, told me after supervising a sprint and hurdles session against his Californian decathlon protégé, England's Barry King, and New Zealand's premier high hurdler, Phil Mills,

"You are ready to run 10.5 for the 100m and 14.6sec for the hurdles."

I was destroying them out of the blocks over 60m. I also ran the first 200m of Jenks's 300m time-trial and recorded a personal best of 21.9sec.

There are a few times in an athlete's career when he or she is really hot, and knows it, you feel it in every sinew. This was my time. In one memorable vault session, the day before the injury scare, I sailed over 5.20m (17ft 1in) at the National Stadium and then put the bar at 5.40m (17ft 8¾in).

I went clear, much to the delight of the hundreds of spectators in the stand.

But now for that 64-dollar question. Would my back stand up? Well I wasn't going to go down without a fight.

The full story is told in a press report;

'The greatest all-round female athlete in the Commonwealth, Mary Peters... and now the greatest all-round male athlete, Mike Bull. He emerged with the decathlon Gold Medal at the end of the second day after 10 tortuous events and sent Northern Ireland's stock sky-high here yesterday.

For sheer guts, stamina and determination this was a magnificent performance by the Belfast lecturer. Remember he started the day 19 points ahead of his nearest rival, but increased his lead to 140 at the finish with a total of 7417 —smashing the old Northern Ireland record by miles.

In between these figures there is drama unequalled when the story of these Games is written. It all began on Sunday last when Mike woke up in bed with muscle spasm – unable to move for two days; "I was told I could forget about competing. But I wanted to go on, and suddenly the pain disappeared as quickly as it had come," he said. He began light training again only on Friday, but was conserving all his energies for Saturday and Sunday.

After he was presented with the Gold, the first to congratulate him was Mary Peters. Both had trained under the late Buster McShane and Mike told me; "It was Buster who first gave me the idea of trying the decathlon. I owe this medal to him." Already telegrams have been pouring into the Ulster headquarters after this major success – a slightly surprising one, for Bull had only competed in a handful of decathlons before. After the Ulster flag had been raised in the stadium Bull sent his love to wife Christina and two-year old son Gavin.

On the dot of 10 o'clock on Sunday morning the second day's events began. In the 110m hurdles Mike came equal first in his heat in 15.3sec, giving him 817

On the top step of the podium for decathlon gold at Christchurch 1974 with silver medalist Barry King on the right and bronze medalist robert Lethbridge behind.
Photo; Stuff Ltd

points. It was an encouraging start for Bull and he was keeping in the medal hunt. Bull moved to top of the table again with his first throw in the discus. Then came Mike's forte – the pole vault. Contemptuously he waited until everyone else was out of the competition before starting. Bull eventually cleared 16ft 5in (5m), enough to give him 1052 points. The Kiwi crowd loved it. They had never seen vaulting like this before. The capacity crowd were generous with their applause, and sympathetic when they saw that Mike was being bothered by the wind. With the javelin and 1500m to come, the big question now was whether the lead was enough – because he knew that these were not his strongest events.

Then came drama in the javelin. Mike injured ligaments in his shoulder with a practice throw. Sean Kyle (NI team coach) managed to get some pain-killing spray out to him and he packed his arm with ice to ease the pain. His first throw was ruled out because he stepped over the line. The second was poor. Would he be beaten at the last hurdle? But his third throw was a personal best and Mike knew in his heart he had won. All he needed to do was complete the 1500m and the Gold Medal was his. He finished second in his heat behind Barry King in 4min 49sec, slow certainly, but after nearly 17 hours of mental and physical exertion, a truly great run. It may have looked ponderous on TV, but it was a performance that will be talked about in Ulster athletics for years.

It was fitting that at the medal presentation all the decathletes who finished the 10 events came out and stood behind the three medalists. An Australian journalist turned to me in the Press box after the band had played the Londonderry Air and said; "How do you Irish do it? The best man and the best woman athlete in the Commonwealth?"

The real answer lies in the months of preparation our golden pair put in during the last 12 months. Then their trip to California and early arrival in Christchurch made the difference between a gold medal and 'also ran'.'

Barry King

Mentioned in the article above, Barry King, who won that exhausting 1500ms final event and thereby secured the silver, was in fact a great friend of mine from Olympic and World Student teams. The same age as myself, we had both been to American universities on athletics scholarships and had a lot in common. He had trained with Mary P and I all throughout the Christchurch Games and with his coach Bill Toomey was a big help to me. After our medal ceremony, where for the first time all the decathletes had formed a circle around the podium, we had hit downtown Christchurch rather hard. At one nightclub a very large man in formal suit approached us with one of his hands held behind his back. Must be a bouncer objecting to our high spirits. He came up to me and I thought 'Trouble', but instead of a fist, from behind he produced a magnum of champagne and said, "Well done Mike. I've followed the event for two days, brilliant. Everything's on the house!" He was the owner of the nightclub, one Fergie McCormick, a truly legendary All-Black and all-round good guy.

We partied the night away, doing justice to the traditions of athletics' all-rounders. Sadly, Barry died on the 27th March 2021 in Colorado Springs near the great Rocky Mountains so beloved of him and wife Deanna. I will always remember him.

The Flag-Bearer

A couple of other things also happened to confirm this period in my life as one of the most fulfilling. I was given the honour of carrying the Northern Ireland flag in the opening ceremony of the Games, which certainly changed my formerly held views about flag-waving at major games – it's OK when it happens to you! In reality, it was a proud moment for me and my family back home.

I also picked up the silver medal in the pole-vault, robbed of Gold by weary legs that had not recovered from the exertions of the decathlon. But as Jenks said to me on the plane home, "I'd give my right arm for any one of those." It had not been a good Games for David.

FATHERHOOD AGAIN

The homecoming was memorable as well. I was awarded my PhD by Queen's University Belfast, having submitted my thesis on Relativism in March. I was promoted to a Senior Lectureship in the department of Sports Studies, which meant Chris could have her new dining room suite.

Oh yes, I almost forgot, baby Natalie was born that May. I couldn't have been away all the time, then!

1974 , my PhD. graduation at Queens University Balfast accompanied by my mother, Anne and heavily pregnant wife Chris

19. Moving On

As Heraclitus said in the 6th century BC "All things are in flux". Advanced years and mounting domestic responsibilities presaged my twilight time in the world of international athletics. I was 30, very old for an athlete in those days and considered high time to start building a sensible, paying career. There had been a few good seasons since the pinnacle of winning two medals at Christchurch and I had managed to amass a British male record of 69 international caps – only beaten recently by the evergreen world record hurdler, Colin Jackson. I had enjoyed my new status as Britain's best all-round athlete and I was nominated captain of our international multi-event team bound for Reykjavic in 1975 (I had to decline as I was back on the pole vault mission by then). I had been, in fact, the first Briton to qualify for the '76 Montreal Olympics with a clearance late in the '75 season of 17ft ¾in (5.20m) at West London.

THE TWILIGHT ZONE WITH THE GOODIES

In '75 I was still acknowledged as Britain's best decathlete and a call from one Bill Oddie (then of the popular TV series *The Goodies* fame) confirmed this. Bill wanted me to be the star of a video he was making for his new record release, *Superspike*, the profits of which were going to the British Olympic team for Montreal. And so, on the appointed day, Bill and I and a film crew of hundreds met at my Wolverhampton club's Aldersley Stadium. In the space of eight hours they filmed me running, hurdling, jumping and throwing all the decathlon events wearing this garish, multi-coloured outfit of our hero, the eponymous Superspike. Bill sang the catchy little song and pretended to climb out of the pit I had just vaulted into and pretended to have released the discus I had just thrown, breasted the tape and so on (you get the picture), as I sprinted from one event to another, completely knackered. It was all great fun though and I did get to make my only appearance on *Top of the Pops* as the tune became a hit record! Be that as it may, the exhausting process tarnished the glamour of becoming a movie star. Besides, by the early stages of 1976 the young kid from Woking was finally coming good.

That shy, awkward little 15 year-old boy who had relentlessly stalked the reception area of the Crystal Palace Hostel all those years ago, finally broke my 10 year-old British pole-vault record. Brian Hooper came to my home track in Belfast (very fitting, I suppose) to jump 17ft 3¼in (5.26m), beating my mark by 0.01m ending my decade as number one.

I still believed that I could come back. However, I was shocked to be informed by the British Board that they were pursuing a 'youth policy' and that myself and a couple of other field event stalwarts, discus champion Bill Tancred and hammer champion Barry Williams, were for the chop and wouldn't be considered for the Montreal Olympics unless we did the standard close to the Games date. The realization was beginning to dawn; the King is dead, long live the King. I was invited to write on the prospect of my demise by *The Guardian* newspaper. What follows is the full text, revealing my state of mind at that time.

MIKE BULL, who pole vaults against Sweden at Edinburgh this weekend, is a Doctor of Philosophy from Queen's University, Belfast. He has been Britain's leading pole vaulter for the past 10 years, taking the British record through 15ft, 16ft, 17ft. Here he discusses the philosophy of his event with ANDREW KITT

CALLED TO THE BAR

IMAGINE standing on top of a 14ft 10in high London bus and falling backwards off it on to a mound of sand a foot deep and flanked by concrete flag stones. Madness: yet for the first of my 10 years in international athletics I was required to perform feats more hazardous than this, stunts which might deter even the redoubtable Evel Knievel. To ride 16 feet of bending glass fibre in strong cross winds to heights in excess of that famous bus, to successfully negotiate a bar placed that high and to land with impunity on a patch of sand which, from that perspective, appears microscopic, is not impossible – myself and others have done it – but it is a dangerous task.

Ask a man why he uses exercise; he will answer because he desires to keep his health. If you then inquire why he desires health, he will readily reply because sickness is painful. If you push your inquiries farther and desire a reason why he hates pain, it is impossible he can ever give any. This is an ultimate end, and is never referred to any other object.

The force of David Hume's words impinges upon the lives, the fears and joys, the aversions and aspirations of a small sub-culture in the world of sport. Human beings have a natural aversion to pain, yet fear of imminent pain is the mode of existence chosen by the pole-vaulter. The esoteric art of defying gravity with 16 feet of fickle glass fibre or with a sturdy length of finely hewn birch, uniquely confronts the agent with the possibility of serious injury. This is my point of departure.

Eros, the life instinct, and Thanatos, the death instinct, live together in an uneasy union within the pole-vaulter. I have nourished these conflicting drives for a decade now and would like to convey the essence of this schizoid life to my fellow man. First I ask for an effort of empathy.

Pole-vaulting is an inherently dangerous activity and bad facilities, which for years haunted British jumpers in this nontraditional event, render it suicidal. Bad facilities excite the mortido, the innate self destructiveness, in vaulters and are the cause of anxiety-neuroses. They have created a monstrous hybrid, the neurotic pole-vaulter. You have seen him, irritatingly hesitant at the end of the runway, pole nervously clenched and unclenched in his agitating hands. The fidgeting fingers of which are being hysterically demanded elsewhere to adjust socks, shorts, and general dishevelment. Eros is fighting back, arguing the case for survival in the face of folly.

Of course nowadays, so the orthodox story goes, things are better. Technology has tenderised the disciples of Icarus, compressed foam-rubber softens our descent from the sun and the spin-offs, from space and aviation research, provide us with high-density and virtually unbreakable poles. With the element of fear thus presumably eliminated, man and bar are perfectly poised. But what about the residues? Of the battered and broken legion from the era of sand and concrete, of soft take-offs and hard landings, I alone am left, bridging however tenuously a generation gap. And all that residual apprehension born of a twice-broken nose, broken wrist and thumb and innumerable near misses still attempts to thwart what the eloquent athletics correspondent of another famous newspaper called 'the vaulting ambition.'

Nevertheless, for the space-age British international vaulter the fear of death is now an anachronism and has been firmly replaced by a new fixation, fear of failure. Fear of failing one's opening height is again uniquely British and has its genesis deeply rooted in our nationalistic pride at scoring points in the dual international meetings which are the real stuff of athletics. It is a syndrome peculiar to vaulting: in running you can lie down, get up and walk home and score a point, in shot-putting the weight can simply fall out of your hand on to the ground six inches in front of you and you score a point.

In vaulting your pole only behaves predictably when you grip it at a specific height (high) run at a specific speed (fast) and take off with a given effort (maximum).

There is no scaling: down to drop over 13ft in order to order to secure that all-important point. Team managers have an uncanny gift for eroding self-belief and lowering the level of aspiration of international vaulters "Get a point first Mike, then go for a big one" usually does the trick.

This systematic perversion of a vaulter's natural individualism eats at his already hard-pressed optimism and the inevitable happens. Fear of failing causes tension and he fails. But this particular anxiety is already on the way out. With the triumph of team management, suggested starting heights for vaulters will soon be low enough to warrant no apprehension, and instead genuine feelings of inferiority will be enjoyed by British international vaulters. They have no right to mimic their Russian rival's jocular refusal of the pole-vault official's invitation to start jumping at five metres (16ft 5in). After all, he is a Russian.

What then comes of a decade defying gravity? The beginnings of self-knowledge and self-identity would, I suppose, be a philosophically respectable answer out modern international sport is an obsession and obsessions cloud reality. Sartre tells us that the first important truth about freedom is that it is unbearable, so perhaps it is understandable that men, in their mauvaise foi, seek an escape in the irrational. Poetry accounts for irrational impulse better than philosophy:

One thousand flights to one thousand places .

One thousand friends won less one thousand faces.

And yet one would hope to have done something worthwhile, to have created something of value in an age of nihilism, to have changed perhaps, in some small way, the attitudes of others. What is to be the criterion of worth however and who is to judge? Is international sport a good thing or is it, in the words of Orwell, "an unfailing cause of ill will... frankly mimic warefare?" Gold medals won and lost balance equally the scales of pain and pleasure.

THE CHANGE

I really enjoyed lecturing, but if you thought the Olympics was competitively tough, the world of academia would make Machiavelli's prince blush. I had been getting to grips with a series of issues in sport and physical education that lent themselves to philosophical analysis. A couple of my papers had been published in peer approved journals and I was invited to present a new paper on 'Practical versus Propositional Knowledge in Sport' to the departmental seminar of the School of Education at Jordanstown. It dealt with the arguments about knowing how to do something as opposed to knowing that something is the case and the widespread belief within physical education that the former was logically independent of and different from the latter. For example,

Mike Bull could know how to pole-vault without knowing about the history, science, mechanics and so on of the event.

The paper was well received by all and sundry and was, after a little sprucing up, submitted to a national physical education journal for publication. Some weeks later, the editor of the journal wrote to me saying how much he enjoyed the article but that he would not be publishing it! Apparently, he had earlier received an almost identical paper with a solution to the problem which was almost the same as mine?

It had been submitted by a highly respected academic from an English university. Who knows what happened; maybe someone had passed on to a friend some notes on a recent paper which may be of interest? What got up my nose was that some of this other person's sentences were barely concealed copies of my own. The similarities were too close to be a coincidence. My head of department, Professor Eric Saunders, later to be Chair of the Sports Council for Northern Ireland, backed up my protests but, in the end, he could only offer the candid viewpoint that such things do happen. Somehow, I thought, I could not see my mentor, Prof Alan Milne, having much truck with this sort of thing.

I was heartily sickened by the thought of some academic simply copying all my months of hard work. I was used to the pure objectivity of a crossbar, either you clear it or you don't, as a measure of success. I did not want any part of this and so, in 1977, at the age of 29 the youngest Senior Lecturer (appointed at age 27) in the college, I told Eric Saunders that I was leaving to open a private gym.

THE GYM PROJECT

On January 29th, 1977, I won my thirteenth and last AAA title in the pole-vault at Cosford, ten years exactly after winning the first.

Three days later, at 10 am sharp, I opened the door to a new life and to Mike Bull's Health Studio in the centre of Bangor, a growing seaside town on the County Down coast some 13 miles from Belfast. Mary P had cut the ribbon at the official Press opening the day before. Now it was the crunch. Would anyone show up for business?

My old school chum, Danny Farrell, and I had been looking at various locations throughout the province which we thought needed a good, multi-purpose, members-only fitness club. Northern Ireland was well provided for in the area of sport and recreation centres. Even in this era there was something like 14 large leisure centres across the province, but there were not many private clubs, on the model of McShane's, catering for regular men and women simply wanting to improve their fitness with a bit of personal supervision. We eventually found excellent premises in a newly constructed first floor showroom in the rapidly expanding seaside dormitory town of Bangor.

It had great potential and there wasn't another comparable gym in the area. One minor problem, Danny was a teacher who drove black taxis at night to make ends meet and, while I may have been famous, there was no money in the sport in those days, so my savings were limited. How were we going to finance it all?

The annual rent for the showroom on a five year lease was £5000, of which the first quarter would have to be up front. The fixtures and fittings, carpets, mirrors, paint (we were painting it ourselves) suspended ceiling and lighting and the construction of a shower area were going to cost a couple of thousand.

Then there was the actual equipment. Danny contacted Victor Coburn, a talented engineer who had made a lot of Buster's apparatus in the days when Danny worked as an instructor at McShane's. Victor churned out the essentials we required to open what, in our own highly contentious words, was to be 'the most modern and best equipped gym in the country'. There were pulley machines, leg machines for quadriceps and hamstrings, calf machines, shoulder and chest apparatus, squat and bench press areas with antique, solid cast-iron, 40lb discs and a full range of barbells and dumbbells. For those less proactive and there were also the 'vibro-massage' belts, units made from washing machines with rapidly shaking canvas belts to 'break down' the fat in those resistant areas? All rather unscientific but extremely popular!

There were great lumps of shining metal which didn't actually do anything but looked impressive. I think Victor eventually charged us about £500 for everything, but I could be wrong, it might have been much less.

Danny and I drove to England in an old camper van to buy a second-hand sauna from a hairdressing salon and dissembled it panel by panel and brought it back on the ferry like an exotic trophy. We also bought a second-hand solarium, really an overhead hanging sunlamp, for we planned to offer free sun tanning to all members in 'the best equipped gym in Ireland.'

A MODEST PROPOSAL

How on earth were we going to pay for all this up front, plus all the usual legal and insurance costs which are inevitable? We were going to need at least £5000.

Danny had saved one thousand pounds and I had about £60 left over from my last pay packet. I did have a lovely little sports car, a blue MGB GT, my pride and joy and a conspicuous feature at local sports meetings with a giant pair of 16ft poles protruding along its tiny roof. Sadly, I sold it for £900 and used fifty of that to buy a horrible old Austin 1100. At least I had wheels, or so I thought; on the way back to Belfast from Bangor one evening something went 'bang' on the flyover road and the car skidded crabwise into the hard shoulder. The axel had snapped and the car that the salesman had described as "the Rolls-Royce of 1100's" met an untimely end. At least we still had the princely capital sum of £1900 with which to impress my bank, the Ulster Bank, on the occasion of my first business proposal to them.

Back in 1974, the Ulster Bank had given a lunch in honour of my Gold medal at Christchurch and the Chairman, Sir Robin Kinnahan, had proffered an open-ended offer of help in any future business ideas I might have. So here I was, in front of the Chairman and his directors, presenting our ambitious plans for the most modern, luxurious health studio with showers, sauna and solarium suite and a fully supervised crèche. Two minutes into my carefully prepared and well-rehearsed presentation (with Danny playing the role of difficult bank manager), Sir Robin interrupted me and asked how much I would need. I apologetically mentioned the exorbitant figure of five grand for establishment costs. The Chairman replied that we would also need something to live on and that he would arrange for an overdraft facility of' £7000 at my local branch!

Deal done! Danny Farrell and Mike Bull were the proprietors of Mike Bull's Health Studio, the Most modern and Best equipped gym in the Universe.

OPEN FOR BUSINESS

I was not a little apprehensive on that opening February morning in 1977. As I unlocked the downstairs glass-fronted door on which was posted a huge, yellow sign bearing the promise,

'FOUNDER MEMBERSHIP OFFER CLOSING SOON'

Danny was busy upstairs. Behind a curtain screening off the training area from the reception, he was still trying to bolt together bits of Victor's unfathomable machines. Meanwhile, my wife, Chris, and newly appointed instructor, Jane Brown, were still painting over the cracks in the wall plaster with magnolia emulsion.

The 'Founder Membership' offer was for one year's membership for £30, or six months for £20, which was probably a little over-priced considering the very few bits of working equipment actually in place and the fact that it was only possible, for the time being, to have a bracing, cold shower. But you could get a tan, or more likely, a bad case of sunburn in the overhanging prototype behind a curtain in the changing room. Danny had engaged a builder who offered to install the showers at an incredibly low cost. However for the opening they had to be turned off because water was leaking into the ground floor premises below, after quite possibly the worst piece of wall and floor tiling in the history of Irish labouring. I remember the builder responsible for the dirty deed had a pronounced limp and I later heard that he'd been knee-capped before his Roy Rogers tiling, so maybe we weren't his first unhappy customer!

"Build it and they will come," as Kevin Costner was told in *Field of Dreams*; and come they did. People started to arrive at the gym. Tom McAuley, my old coach, was one of the first to sign on for the year and,

Build it and they will come?
Photo: Belfast Telegraph Archive

although he never actually managed to train at the club, he did renew his membership for years thereafter. This phenomenon was repeated hundreds of times over the next 25 years, confirming my belief that it is often the physical act of joining (and paying for) a gym that can be good for you. All that guilt instantly unloaded by the simple swish of a cheque-book and pen.

People came in their droves. Mr & Mrs Kane, a well established Bangor family, enrolled at least ten members of their large, extended family. Young mothers came in that morning, deposited their screaming kids in the crèche with Diane (our crèche minder and future long term instructor) and escaped for an hour or so of verbal calisthenics of their own- yes, there was lots of talk! Shift workers arrived from all-night duty for a bit of exercise. Unemployed men joined the club to pass a hitherto unproductive day. Policemen, solicitors, barristers, judges, known paramilitaries, convicted killers (I kid you not), men of the cloth, TV personalities and

First Health & Beauty—

Get in Shape at Mike Bull's Belfast and Bangor Gyms

Mike Bull's fitness and health clubs offer a complete range of superb facilities, with new Powersport Guardian resistance machines, cardiovascular steppers, cycles, rowers and joggers, as well as male and female saunas and RUVA sunbeds. Nutritional advice is available, and you can enjoy refreshments at the reception bar. To introduce his health facilities to First Card News readers, Mike is offering a prize of a 3-month membership, at his Belfast or Bangor locations to two First Card News winners.

To enter this competition, tick the box on our First Reply coupon on page 7, and send it back today!

sportsmen and women of all types enrolled in 'the best equipped gym in Europe.'

By the end of the first day we had an amazing 200 members. We could, had we wanted, paid off the bank loan in the first few hours of business. Only one person was given their money back, the only member with genuine psychopathic tendencies that we ever had the privilege of meeting. This chap was doing barbell curls in front of one of the wall-mounted mirrors when suddenly, shrieking a Kung-Fu sort of warrior cry, he hurled the barbell at the wall and leaped commando-like over a bench in readiness for an imaginary enemy! Danny called him calmly into our little office and, in a monument to self-restraint, while writing out a cheque for a full refund of the maniac's membership fee, said, "Good luck in your next gym," and threw his clothes and training bag down the stairs. Buster would have been proud of him.

The gym was such a success that by the end of the first year we had opened another, this time in Ballymena. This rural County Antrim town had a great sporting tradition and matched all the criteria that we had set for Bangor, except that is, for its reputation in business circles of being hard on 'blow-ins' (outsiders) together with a Scottish propensity for penury (the land of the Ulster Scots). Hard and penurious was certainly our experience of Ballymena for the single year of the new gym's duration, after which we sold out and quit while we were at least even.

Business in Bangor continued to expand, to the extent that at one stage we had four part-time instructors working for us. One great story concerns a young English Lad who had moved to Northern Ireland and joined the Gym. He had no job and no real place of his own to live but he did very well at the training and had a nice, easy-going way about him. I offered him a few hours a week instructing at busy periods in the Gym, paying him about £1 an hour. I also gave him a bed on the floor of our spare room at home to tide him over – and no, I did not charge him. His name was Alan Nappin, who became the millionaire owner of electrical manufacturers and suppliers with factories in Belfast, Warrington and China!

Alan is still a great friend, even though I persist in introducing him as a "former employee of mine." I also delight in passing around the old photographs of him complete with muscles and six-pack. There have been a few six-packs under the bridge since then!

Soon after this, Danny's itching feet made the far- away fields of Australia look greener and he decided to sell up and emigrate south, very south. We agreed on a financial settlement and I re-financed my car, took out a business loan and a second mortgage on our home. I was now sole owner of the gym.

20. SUPERSTARS

In the 80's one of the most popular shows on television was *Superstars*. The format was simple; invite a group of sports champions each week to compete against one another in a selection of unfamiliar sporting activities, offer prize money to make it competitive and hold a grand final, to be screened at peak viewing time on national TV.

Local Superstars in Bangor N I L-R Maurice Foster, me , Brian Hooper

It had worked well in the States with Olympic vault champion, Bob Seagren, winning the inaugural final in great style. Kjell Isaksson won the European version and then Brian Hooper kept it in the vault family by taking the whole series by storm. Brian, with his analytical approach to perfecting his technique and his impressive strength-to-bodyweight ratio, set new standards in the contest which eclipsed the early stars like Canada's Brian Budd and England's Olympic judo star, Brian Jacks. Hoops won the World Superstars two years in succession and won himself a tidy sum in the dollars for points arrangement. Unfortunately, this tidy sum was tidily swindled from him by a thieving financial agent and Brian eventually went back to vaulting. However, by this time his best jumping days were behind him and the Superstars bubble was beginning to burst – though not, thankfully, before yours truly was invited on to the scene in 1985 by the BBC and Mark McCormack's sports agency to compete in the Past Masters Superstars.

THE BBC TV SUPERSTARS

Along with the likes of sporting legends such as West Ham's Billy Bonds, Welsh and Lions rugby international Phil Bennett, British 400m hurdles champion Bill Hartley, Commonwealth and European marathon champion Ian Thompson, international cricketer Graham Rupe and World boxing champion John H. Stracey, I accepted the challenge to pit our wits and fitness over three days of physical activity. There was swimming, sprinting, an 800m run, weightlifting, combat pistol shooting, golf, gym tests and the famous obstacle course. I was ruled out of the 60m sprint as being too similar to my specialist sport, which I thought odd in view of the fact that both Bill Hartley, an international 'sprinter' and Phil Bennett, a 'sprinting' back in rugby, filled the first and second places in that event.

I did, however, come good in the swimming, those hours spent in the Falls Road Baths finally paying off. I was also, surprisingly, unbeatable in the pistol shooting, having been tutored by a certain Brian Hooper in the finer points of breathing and pointing. In the weightlifting I just didn't need help from any quarter and won easily. In the final act, the whole contest came down to a head-to-head over the obstacle course between me and fellow international athlete, Bill Hartley. The prize was the Townsend Torenson Superstars trophy and a few thousand pounds.

I have to admit that I had taken the whole competition quite seriously, not so much because of the prize money or the celebrity status guaranteed to the winner, but rather because Seagren, Isaksson and Hooper had established the all- round supremacy myth of the pole-vaulter. I felt that I had to win. Not everyone felt the same way. John H. Stracey was a wonderful character who between camera shooting locations did his best to emulate Arthur Daley; from the boot of his car John sold the finest sports and leisure gear, after shave, perfume, you name it, John H. sold it. I invested heavily in an Italian designer sports shirt, genuine article you understand.

Back to that final head-to-head. Pole-vaulters were born for events like swinging on a rope over a wall, vaulting over a box, hand-walking across parallel bars, running along a balance beam and finishing off with a front somersault over a crossbar on to a mat. This was the obstacle course and the difference between first and second place was some £1500... I won! Ron Pickering enjoyed the post-match interview with the exhausted victor (myself) and I enjoyed my first ever official professional sports fee.

WORLD SUPERSTARS

The spin-offs from all this, the personal appearances and sports-related events which came my way as a result of prime-time television exposure and a sponsored Audi sports car, gave me a whole new lease of life in this strange, sporting sub-species some insightful commentators called 'trash- sport.' Trash or not, a third place in the World Superstars Final in Cyprus was a lot of fun in the sun with an illustrious cast, including even-tual winner the youthful Robin Brew, GB Olympic swim captain, Olympic Champions Victor Davies (Canada, swimming), Ralf Darrendorf (Germany, discus), and Ian Thompson (New Zealand, kayak), World 400m Champion Bert Cameron (Jamaica), World Triathlon Champion Mark Allen and Ireland kayak international Alan Bates. In the end it was quite an experience and it earned me a few more quid for the pension pot.

Some of the World Superstars Cyprus 1985. L-R (back): Alan Bates, Victor Davies, Mark Allen, Robin Brew. front; Ian Ferguson, Brian Hooper (reigning world superstars champion) & me

I was just beginning to like this professional sport business when television decided to pull the plug on the long running series, and it was all over as quickly as it had begun. I did, however, manage to secure a permanent legacy from this period as a sporting mercenary – I bought a small apartment in Southern Spain, from where I started writing this manuscript some 18 years later, and which I still own to this day.

SPARKS FLY

One splendid consequence of my higher profile as a 'TV personality' was that it got a lady called Karen Girvan (now a real Lady) to thinking strategically. Karen, a barrister out of Queen's University, joined the Gym for two reasons; a) to get fit and, b) to talk me into establishing with her a Northern Ireland branch of the sports charity, *Sport Aiding Research into Krippling Diseases* (SPARKS). She thought that with the help of a high- profile launch and lots of media coverage we could together raise a pile of money for medical research into the sort of crippling diseases that prevented young people from ever getting the chance to participate in sport.

In 1986, with the full help and co-operation of the Sports Council for Northern Ireland and its then chief executive, George Glasgow, SPARKS Northern Ireland was launched on an unsuspecting public. A committee was formed comprising Adrienne Catherwood (the first and most revered local TV presenter) as President, TV sports presenter Mark Robson as Vice Chairman, Karen as Secretary, and members including high jumper Janet Boyle, bowler Freda Elliott, rugby's

Mike Gibson, lawyer and gaelic footballer Eugene Grant, rally driver Drew Wylie, golf champion David Young, rugby international Trevor Ringland, cricket international Dermott Monteith, Olympic decathlete Colin Boreham, with the tireless organizer Pam Anstey, and myself as Chairman.

After chairing this lot of sporting icons for some 16 years, I at last stood down to allow Ulster Television presenter, Pamela Ballantine, to take the Chair in 2002, but most of the same faces are still there on the committee or acting as patrons and still raising thousands of pounds every year for medical research.

Karen, now Lady Girvan, was my rock in all the charity's efforts. I was, as she used to say, "Our Leader". I kind of miss that.

21. DEATH AND TAXES

The First Principle of the human condition states that the only certainty is death and taxes. Life was eventually to test its fundamental law on me.

THE TELEVISION YEARS

During the heyday of the Superstars mania in the early 80s, Terry Smith, the genial Sports Editor of Ulster Television, approached me for my ideas on an ambitious new programme he was producing for the autumn schedule. It was to be based on the tried and trusted multi-sports formula, except that it was designed to pit one sport against another in a more direct and confrontational way. It would raise an issue that was truly irresistible to the very factional thinking of the average Northern Irish armchair athlete, 'Who are the best all-round athletes, rugby, soccer or gaelic players?'

Terry and I designed many of the sporting challenges, the usual mix of speed, strength and endurance tests, in the wee coffee shop beside the Gym. We also added an element of daring-do in what would be the final challenge, the obstacle course. This would reach its climax with a canoe race across a Lake, the scaling of a forty- foot tower of scaffolding and a hair-raising abseil slide, with competitors hanging on to overhead pulley-handles, down a rope stretched 300m from the top of the tower to the ground on the far side of the lake.

Our ambitious designs were facilitated by the choice of the wonderfully scenic Lakeland Forum in Enniskillen, in the heartland of Fermanagh's beautiful lake district, as our venue. There was endless scope for water sports, running events, cycle trails, ball games and everything else we could dream up to throw at the competitors. And then there was Rodney Connor, the local director of recreation, who in his own mischievous way, was willing to move heaven and earth to support the event... which was just as well as this turned out to be the exact requirement!

I was to be the co-presenter and commentator for the series along with UTV's then 'Mr Sport', Jackie Fullerton, in what was to be the start of a long-running partnership. Jackie, himself a local soccer star of the dim and distant past (that's not fair but I know it'll get him going), did a great job in holding the show together and in teaching his new apprentice (me) a few old tricks. It wasn't always easy for him to baby sit me but at least I sometimes made him laugh.

Jackie's fabled smoothness and sense of humour were severely tested by my ineptitude and ham-fistedness on many occasions. During one of the earlier programmes we were to do a post-competition summary to camera, and we had set marks to walk to and set pieces-to-camera to speak and a short head to head discussion of proceedings.

Under the direction of series director, Alan Hailes (or King Vidor as Jack called him), I was given a hand-held microphone and my lines to learn.

I emerged from our commentary suite, in reality an old caravan heavily stocked with our sponsor's milk products and the odd bottle of Bacardi, word perfect and ready to emulate Dean's vestigial performance in *East of Eden*. I hit my mark perfectly, waited my cue, said my little piece with surprising poise and then launched enthusiastically into a meaningful discussion on the pros and cons of rugby and gaelic football with a bemused looking Jackie.

Jackie, the old pro that he is, looked me straight in the eyes and with great sincerity asked, "Yes Mike, I agree... but I was wondering what is that you're holding in your right hand?"

I glanced down at my knuckle-white right hand by my thigh and the tightly clenched black, furry object in its grasp. We both burst out laughing as Alan shouted "Cut" – I was so nervous and was concentrating so hard on walking up and hitting my chalk mark and saying my lines that I had forgotten to raise my microphone towards my mouth when speaking! As Jackie said, "Now you'll appreciate just how difficult it is for John Wayne to walk that walk and say the lines in front of camera." Take two!

Filming the lakeland games with Margaret Harper and TV crew

The *Lakeland Games*, as the series was called, became enormously popular, certainly one of the most popular home produced programmes ever in the Province. The series ran for about four years with ever more intricate versions of that vexatious old question of whether gaelic's Mickey-Joe would beat rugby's Willie-John at gym tests. I think it eventually ended when Terry really just grew exhausted running around trying to please scores of temperamental sportsmen and women.

It certainly could be difficult handling the different personalities. Terry once asked me to intervene and speak strongly to one competitor from a contact sport who had publicly berated a tremulous female team-mate, who just also happened to be the sportsman's girlfriend, for chickening out on top of the tower when faced with the nail-biting, hanging slide over the lake. I mean, the poor girl was simply terrified of heights and this guy was almost pushing her off the 40 foot tower. No head for heights, eh, grounds for divorce I'd say.

Next, UTV asked me to be main commentator of an annual International Basketball tournament, which was one of the most difficult jobs I was to undertake; all that unfamiliar terminology and all the fast action to follow. I had only my experience of selling programmes and popcorn at collegiate ball games at Southern Illinois University to fall back on. Indeed, if I remember correctly, it was precisely this heady background in the sport which persuaded Terry Smith to give me a shot at the commentary. Jackie unsympathetically told me if I thought that was difficult, try commentating on Northern Ireland v. Albania in soccer, note-less and director-less from a dugout in Tirana!

It is undoubtedly true that sportspersons who have the knack for it find the world of television broadcasting congenial, not too far removed from the field of sport in terms of adrenaline rush and ego gratification. I really enjoyed it and apparently had sufficient knack to get away with it. I was then given a regular five minute health and fitness slot on Gerry Kelly's long running consumer affairs teatime show, *Lifestyle*. Ulster Television also commissioned me to write a Lifestyle Fitness Manual to accompany the programme, which I did but the plug was pulled on the series before the book could be published.

That's the trouble with the wonderfully profligate world of television, you never know what's going to happen next. Gerry and I had received good reviews from the critics on the fitness format I had devised about the simplest and most convenient ways for 'the man in the street' to get fit. Again, I think Gerry had really had quite enough of the programme; the floor director would invariably be shouting for Kelly during one of his very occasional smoking breaks, "Gerry, Lifestyle Fitness ready to record." Spitting out the inhaled toxic fumes, Kelly would growl, "Lifestyle is it, you mean effin' Lifes-bore!" My guess is he'd had enough.

My mini-career in television was really blossoming what with all this and a regular spot on a new UTV game show called *Password*, and lots of other little projects in between, like Ron Pickering's *We Are The Champions*. I was doing quite well, in a fairly harmless sort of way… but someone was watching who did not like it at all.

THE FERRYMAN

According to the taxman, someone telephoned anonymously, alleging that I had a fortune stashed in some offshore bank, that I owned a luxury villa in Marbella and had countless pots of gold buried all over the place! I had none of the above, but thanks to Superstars I did have my wee, one-bedroom apartment in Malaga and some modest stock-market shares.

In the end I had to pay back-tax due on the various prize monies and for the interest on the investments going back some ten years, a tidy sum in all.

It was apparently something of a moral victory for me as it was the smallest punishment allowable under the circumstances. Culpability could have meant 100% penalty. I now know why Al Capone cracked.

But that wasn't the end of the affair. There is another immutable law of human social living, nicely summed up by that timeless sage Bertie Wooster; "It's always just when a fellow is feeling particularly braced with things in general that Fate sneaks up behind him with the bit of lead piping." The codicil to this states that, During Times of Adversity there is One Thing to Fear more than the Taxman – the VAT man. The good Inspector had raised the possibility that he might have to inform the VAT people about my newfound financial status since I may have exceeded the threshold making me liable for this tax. On the other hand, as it was matter-of-factly put, he may not have to. He would let me know. As you might have guessed, no slack was cut and I faced the terrifying prospect of owing 17% of everything I had earned, Gym and all, over the past ten years. Don't you just love the casual, diceman-like manner of their decision whether or not to bankrupt someone and ruin several lives?

I don't mind admitting that I was worried. I even went back to St. Malachy's Chapel, behind Belfast's City Hall, and recited that often voiced prayer of the agnostic which always begins, "If there's anyone up there…". I am sure the Catholic Church has an appropriate saint to address the problem of the VAT man, but my mother wasn't around to consult on the matter. In the absence of divine intervention, I faced ruin. And then it happened, divine intervention I mean, in the rather unconventional form of the Belfast Telegraph.

One evening my attention was drawn to an article in the newspaper. Apparently there was European legislation which provided for the exemption of teachers in the business of teaching subjects ordinarily taught on the curriculum of schools and colleges, no matter where the teaching takes place. Physical Education was such a subject, ergo, the business was exempt. BINGO!

Propelled into action with all the energy and determination of an Olympian, I prepared a defence for my accountant along the same lines. I was a qualified teacher teaching an element of physical education in a private gym and was therefore not liable to pay VAT. Unfortunately, they did not just take my word for it. An Inspector was assigned to the case, naturally.

The new Inspector instructed myself and my accountant to be available every day for a month in the Gym between 9am and 11am so that he could observe me working in the Gym. That being done, some impenetrable calculation was forthcoming, based on the proportion of my time at work spent on non-physical education activities, like talking on the phone, administration, hoovering, cleaning the showers, polishing the mirrors and God knows what. I tried to explain that it was impossible to separate my 'teaching' from my 'observing' the members on the gym floor and that, indeed, I could observe and talk on the phone at the same time. The inquisitor, sorry Inspector, seemed unconvinced but it quickly became obvious that the whole calculus idea was ridiculous. It was still produced, and I won the case. It was, however, a Pyrrhic victory. My accountancy bill (mitigated by my accountant and old school classmate and friend Gerry Prior) for all those hours in the gym was presented, at the statutory rate of £45 an hour PLUS VAT!

I had to pay it all. I'm surprised I didn't have to pay the inquisitor's salary for the period. It's true what they say, you know, you really can't win. You are drowning slowly in the water, but The Ferryman Also Must Be Paid. But at last I was completely exonerated.

The Taxman was not the only one looking his dues. Between 1995 and 2002 I was to lose most of my immediate family; mother, father, wife, half brother and sister all crossed that Stygian divide. I had reached that stage in life when, as my father had always complained, "the only time I wear a suit is for a funeral."

My mother had been talking for some time about a pain in her heel which was beginning to interfere with her daily swimming, yoga, tennis, hairdressing for the neighbours and visiting the sick and infirm. She was eighty two.

The consultant Oncologist, an Old Malachian of similar vintage to myself, confirmed to a tearful husband and son that Anne Bull, nee

McKee, from County Armagh, had between six months and a year at the outside to live, due to a tumour on the psoas. And we were thinking it was some sort of sports injury. As mother had always been one to extract the full value of a dealt hand, she lasted a further gruelling fifteen months.

This first chink in the armour plating of our family's hitherto impregnably fit-and-heathy vanguard hit father pretty hard. He himself was in the middle of studying for his BA in Humanities at Queen's University and preparing for his normal appearance in the Irish Triathlon Championships. But then he was only 76. However, when the Ferryman starts touting for business, he really sticks the boot in.

Returning to their Cavehill Road home in North Belfast after a Mother's Day dinner with us in Bangor, a celebration mother had been too ill to attend, dad's car was hit by a speeding fire engine. He had to be cut from the wreckage.

I got to the Royal Victoria Hospital, in all its enduring Victorian splendour, within an hour of the accident, in good time to pass the mangled wreck being winched up on a crane on the Belfast Road. How could anyone survive that? But survive he did, along with my half brother Hugh and his wife Vera, with no visible wounds on his body that I could see. In the emergency room dad's only inquiry was regarding the status of his legs, no doubt with that triathlon still in mind. I checked under the sheet and told him they were fine, as indeed they were, but with a broken sternum, 14 broken ribs, a punctured heart and lung and impending renal failure, the legs were the only thing in good shape.

Dad somehow survived the 15 days and nights in intensive care, where there is actually no distinction between day and night, his speech peculiarly reverting to the West Country vernacular of a boy sailor that had been completely camouflaged by a lifetime in Northern Ireland. At one time, close to death, he saw the white light at the end of the tunnel, the picket fence and the familiar faces of long-gone relatives on the other side. He was refused admission this time and came back in time to bury his wife, the saddest day of his life, and to get his university degree, the proudest. He did not, to his eternal regret, get to compete in that triathlon.

1977, dad graduating from Queens with his BA aged 77.

On the eve of Christmas 2000, we sat by a roaring log fire in my house and watched the sadly shaking figure of Muhammed Ali on Sports Review of the Year. Dad then got up and left, heading to his bungalow in our back-garden with a hint of moisture in his eye. He had always admired the sheer athleticism of Ali, "Quicker than Joe Louis," he would say, "but not as hard a puncher." I caught a glimpse of him the following frosty morning on his way to the swimming pool for his usual swim session. It was to be my final glimpse.

My niece Christina was on the phone to me an hour later from the swimming pool where she managed the leisure complex, "Come quickly, your father's had an accident."

As I entered the pool deck it was all over. John Bull's 6 foot long, athletic body was lying on its back on the cold, wet tiles, like a warrior on his shield. His battered and bruised heart had simply given up mid stroke and the old man of the sea had died instantly in the medium that best befitted him. There would be no more battles for Chief Petty Officer F.W.J. Bull, BA

22. LE RUGBY

"Mike, the Ireland selectors have told me to gain a stone. I'm too small."

Thus Mark McCall, the captain of the 1999 European Cup winning Ulster rugby team and Ireland international, made his introduction at the Bangor gym and hence the enduring nickname of the present Saracens Head Coach, 'Smallie'.

The gyms in Bangor and Belfast[1] had become a focal point for ambitious sportsmen and women from all over the province. It had helped that I was still getting sporting headlines.

BULL STILL KING AT 44

– proclaimed the leading Sunday newspaper in the province when I won the Irish pole-vault championship at Morton Stadium, formerly Santry, in Dublin. Since I had won the Northern Irish title the previous week, I was being hailed as the champion of All-Ireland.

I also entered, during that same year of '91, the World Masters Athletics Championships in Turku, Finland. I was really enjoying this fantasy world of so-called 'big time' athletics at an age when most people knew better. The Press and the sporting public seemed to love it, spurred on by stories of Mark Spitz making a comeback and so on. The world of instant telecommunications made it all different from the remote and distant theatres of Mexico '68 and all that, so I suppose the armchair athletes could readily feast their fantasies on the likes of the mythical Spitz and myself. At any rate, I won and became a World Champion.

---

1   I had opened the latter in '93 as a consequence of an IRA bomb which temporarily destroyed the Bangor premises, and closed it in '97 as a consequence of the residual fear and apprehension which made central Belfast a 'ghost town' every evening after 7pm

I was undeniably in great physical shape. For many years I had been doing an early Sunday morning running session in Bangor Castle Park, close to the Gym, followed by an endurance circuit in the Gym. At the outset, I'd do the session by myself and just push out the envelope as far as I could in every activity I chose for the morning. Chris got used to my Sunday afternoons (the Gym closed at 2 o'clock) sprawled out on the sofa. I was training hard every day and eating in the 'Zone'.

MIKE GIBSON AND THE DIRTY DOZEN

Then some guys and girls in the Gym who were keen on general Sports fitness including Mark Redden, John Mitchell and John McKinley started doing the training with me. No matter how hard I pushed, whatever ridiculously impossible work-loads I imposed, these Dirty Dozen (sometimes more than twelve in number but always sweaty and mucky) were right there, and they did it too. Certainly, at one stage they were as good as most international athletes in terms of general conditioning. Then the legendary Irish and British Lion rugby player, Mike Gibson, joined the group. Mike loved it. I had done some interval running sessions with him before on the track during my decathlon days and I soon discovered that Mike had lost none of his passion for fitness. In his playing days, apart from his natural vision and skill, not to mention a withering side-step, his game had always displayed a huge, slow beating engine for his cardio-vascular system. He was the type of player, much like Brian Robson or Roy Keane in soccer, who could quite simply run all day long… but Mike had <u>never</u> done any weight-training!

Talk about a duck to water, within a couple of months of starting my weights schedule, his thighs and upper torso were bursting with eight pounds of extra lean muscle. Mike would grab me by the arm and squeeze hard, declaring, "If I'd done this sooner, I'd still be playing for Ireland."

I would smile knowingly and unflinching, pretending the squeeze didn't hurt.

Mike Gibson still works out, although with a little less ferocity, and always features in the pundits' world all-time-team selection, a fitting tribute to the greatest of players. However, it wasn't only rugby players who gravitated to the Gym, for in the '80s and '90s most sports began to recognize the necessity for specialist strength-training and conditioning. Swimming and boxing were the last great bastions of resistance to the value of weight training and then along came Mark Foster and Michelle Smith and boxers Barry McGuigan and Steve Collins.

At different times, McGuigan and Collins lived in a guest house in Bangor, run by Jean Anderson, just around the corner from the Gym. I knew Barry well enough from his amateur days in the Commonwealth Games team and from the Irish Superstars, where he demonstrated great power and technique in the weightlifting. Barry only used my gym on the rare days he had off from the rigorous schedule imposed at Barney Eastwood's boxing gym.

Steve Collins, however, was different; he was a real gym rat. Quiet and modest in those days, he started training anonymously in the evenings at the club. I didn't know him at all, but I did notice the hundreds of weighted sit-ups and crunches and the thirty minutes he would spend on special strengthening exercises for his neck muscles. As anyone who followed his fights will know, he could take a good punch to either head or body.

He would also work hard on his bench-pressing for upper body strength. One evening, as I was spotting for him at the bench, he calmly told me that he was going to New York to fight an American for the World Middleweight title, and he intimated that this would provide financial security for his wife and children. I must admit I was impressed, but not as much as by the fight itself. Steve only lost the decision by the narrowest of point margins in what was hailed as one of the best ever performances by a middleweight from these islands. He went on, of course, to beat Chris Eubank for the World title and to international fame amid a complete change of personality that had him playing at mind games and hypnotism with opponents. Whatever it takes, man, whatever it takes.

As for the sport of swimming, there was a prevalent prejudice in Irish circles that only very light weights and high repetition, circuit-type training was of any value. I had always argued that such endurance work was already being done in the long hours of pool training, and that the gym was the place to prioritize strength training, heavier weights and less repetitions.

Ashley Morrison, the great former Irish butterfly record holder from Carrowdore in North Down, came back from a sports scholarship in Houston, Texas, to train with me for the Commonwealth Games. He was accustomed to the hard, heavy weights of the US system and he flourished at my Gym, winning Ulster and Irish championships and making the Commonwealth Games team.

Buster McShane had embraced the same principles of strength training for swimming when working with Andy Hunter, who set a long-standing 100m freestyle record for Ireland and who gained selection for Ireland in the Munich Olympics. In recent times, I have enjoyed great satisfaction in training his son, Andy junior, for strength and conditioning, eventually seeing the younger generation beating the father's times.

Many sports were represented at the Gym. Two young lads, just finished with school, were brought to see me by their father, full of hope and ambition for his sons who had just been given apprenticeships at Manchester United. They were both talented and hard-working but neither graduated successfully from that Old Trafford wringer. It really emphasized the fact that so few of these young soccer hopefuls ever make the big time. Today, my own 18-year-old grandson, Max, is in a similar position.

Sports persons from all over the province were regularly coming to the Gym sessions; promising athletes, hockey players, martial arts exponents from as far away as Larne, most of the Belfast Royal Academy school rugby team and quite a few of the Ulster Badminton squad. Some Sunday mornings, there could be more than twenty turning up at the park for the 20m bleep test shuttle run, interval training and plyometric hopping, bounding and jumping over hurdles. Mark McCall was one of these and soon started lifting weights with me three evenings a week on a progressive resistance programme that visibly packed muscle on to his slender frame.

I advocated, and still do, a modified 'Zone' eating regime where particular attention is paid to balancing the usually (in Northern Ireland) high carbohydrate intake with a near equal amount of high-quality protein. It worked well for Mark, gaining for him both that required stone in bodyweight and a reputation as a ferociously hard tackler. He turned out to be a pretty good coach too with the rather successful Saracens team!

ULSTER EXPECTS

One day, Mark informed me that Ulster Rugby were advertising for a full-time Fitness Coach to be based at the famous Ravenhill Grounds. I applied, was interviewed by Ulster Coach, Harry Williams, and team Manager, John Kinnear, and got the job.

I jumped straight in, organizing the day to day training sessions for the 25 professionals in my charge. Morning speed-endurance at the Mary Peters Track, endurance work in the fields and hills surrounding, afternoon weights at the Ravenhill gym which I was equipping to become one of the finest weight areas in the country, circuit training for local muscular endurance and pool recovery sessions at the University.

I quickly discovered that not everyone was equally enthusiastic about the swimming pool element. David Humphreys, star playmaker for Ulster and Ireland, made it clear to me that he hated water, unless he was drinking it, and not to expect him too often at the baths. To be fair, he did make a big effort and splashed about occasionally, more as an example to the other resisters than anything else.

Nor was the short-recovery interval running to everyone's liking. Mark 'Blairso' Blair, a big 6ft 6in (2m), 17½ stone (120kg) second-row forward, not ideally built for middle-distance running, actually lay down on the grass during one hard work-out and, hands behind his head in reclining pose, declared, "That's it, no more bloody running for me!"

He didn't get much sympathy from 'Clarkie' (Alan Clarke) or 'Boat' (Gary Longwell), the two hardest-working soldiers in the pack. I think they actually fined him a pound for non-compliance, but then that didn't mean much since everything was liable to attract a fine. I was once fined a pound for being too enthusiastic, and 'Big Ron', coach Harry Williams, was fined a pound for being 2 minutes late at the airport – he had been stopped for speeding en route by the police and only by luck had he escaped a ticket. He did not have similar fortune with the lads. He was given another pound fine for concocting such a lame excuse!

They were a great bunch to work with, real pioneers of the professional era in rugby and determined to maintain their newfound status at the top of Europe. 'Humph (David Humphreys) was the model pro, very single-minded and confident of his playing skills. He quickly realized that he needed to be stronger and faster and applied himself diligently, and successfully, to this end.

There were some excellent natural athletes among the squad, the sort of talented young men who could have done well in any number of sports. Andy 'Wardie' Ward, the big naturalized New Zealander who had spells as team captain, and Johnnie 'Dinger' Bell were both extremely strong on weights, quick and good endurance runners as well. Andy's continued neglect at the hands of the Ireland selectors was totally inexplicable, unless you are one of the insiders who understands the prejudices of the so-called Munster 'Mafia.'

Wardie wasn't the only good player to be overlooked for international selection; brilliant wingers like James Topping and Tyrone Howe have in the past been ignored as well. At one stage Tyrone was picked for the British Lions, the greatest representative honour available, yet overlooked for Ireland.

The worst case of this was probably the player who was the undoubted star of that great Ulster team. Simon 'Macey' Mason had won the European Cup for us by becoming the leading kicker and points scorer in Europe. Macey did not exactly relish the crunching tackle, especially when it was on himself, but give him a shot on goal from anywhere within 50 or 60 yards and you could guarantee three points. I think he got one single Ireland cap. He couldn't understand why Warren Gatland, the famous Irish Coach at the time, would not pick him but, as I was to eventually find out, Warren probably did not have much of a say in it. Big Ron at any rate would always put Simon's name down first on the team sheet, saying of the Irish Liverpudlian, "He wins matches for us."

IRELANDS CALL

Harry Williams decided to retire at the end of his contract period with Ulster. A South African, Alan Solomons, was appointed as the new manager and he made it clear that he was bringing his own fitness coach with him. Despite the fact that I had a year of my own contract to go, I was paid off and resolved to concentrate my efforts in the future of the Gym in Bangor. However, I received a surprise phone call from the Director of Fitness for Ireland Rugby at Lansdowne Road. Liam Hennessey was the name and he was incensed at the way I had been ousted from the Ulster set-up, but he really took me by surprise when he said, "The Ireland job has become available. We would like you to take it." I pretended to remain cool and told him I would sleep on it but in my mind's eye I was already the Ireland Fitness Coach. I accepted the following day. A newspaper reported the story;

IRISH TAKE BULL BY THE HORNS

Mike Bull, arguably Ireland's most successful athlete of all time, is taking on a new challenge- as Irish rugby's National Fitness Adviser.

The man who set new standards for British pole-vaulting in the 1960s and 70s, and then went on to become an international decathlete, has had an equally impressive career since retirement from competition.

He built up a hugely successful gymnasium business over the years and he's been involved in helping literally hundreds of sportsmen and women to prepare properly for top-class action in various sports.

Bull is highly regarded for his innovative approach to personal fitness, and his involvement with the Ulster rugby team in recent years has won the unanimous approval of players and management alike. He had intended to take a less prominent role in rugby matters, and had stepped down from his Ravenhill post when new coach Alan Solomons was appointed. The man filling his shoes as Ulster's fitness guru is Solomons' fellow South African Phil Mack.

But the decision of the current adviser to Warren Gotland and the Irish national management and coaching staff, Craig White, to resign to take up a similar role at Premiership soccer outfit Bolton Wanderers opened a door Bull had never expected.

Bull has, in a packed 56 years, been an Olympic athlete, a Commonwealth Games gold medallist, an influential academic, and a successful businessman. Even now he competes on the international stage at Veterans' level, frequently setting new benchmarks in several disciplines, including the pole vault.

As a young man he won a scholarship to the United States, and on his return to Northern Ireland he was one of the most recognisable faces in sport. He famously trained for his specialist event in the cavernous but hardly state -of -the -art warehouses at Harland and Wolff.

With Mary Peters he dominated Ulster athletics, and the pair brought back Gold from the Commonwealth Games in Edinburgh in 1970. Bull completed his studies and earned his doctorate, and after retiring from top-class athletics he lectured at the University of Ulster. In parallel he founded his successful gym in Bangor and that has over the last three decades been a Mecca for aspiring competitors in all sporting disciplines.

I was responsible for all the pre-match fitness training of the Ireland Rugby Team, their diet and nutrition, their day-to-day bodyweight, their preparation and warm-up before the matches and their post-game recovery sessions. But first I had to meet the team, and this was scheduled for the two-week training camp in July 2001 at Spala, near Warsaw, in Poland.

Spala was a superb, purpose-built training complex in the middle of the Polish countryside, very remote and very removed from social distractions. The heart of the camp was the splendid 400m track, surrounded by wooded flatlands with extensive running trails and studded by hotel-standard living quarters and a fine self-service restaurant. There was also a full international indoor track with comprehensive weight- lifting and weight training areas and dozens of Olympic barbells and thousands of kilos of weight.

There was also a nice 25m pool, just to keep David Humphreys happy, and also a facility which was to be the focal point of the two weeks. It was called a Cryotherapy Unit.

TILL HELL FREEZES OVER

The IRFU Director of Fitness, Liam Hennessy, himself a former ex-Irish pole-vault champion (you can't get away from these pole-vaulters), was highly interested in the use of ice and cold water in aiding the recovery of sportsmen after heavy training and competition. Dr Hennessy had already introduced the most unpopular ritual in the history of Irish sport, the post -match wheelie-bin dip. In the bowels of the Lansdowne Road shower area he had installed a couple of industrial sized plastic bins, filled with crushed ice and very cold water. After the game, each player had to line up and sit totally immersed in the icy bath for an eternal two minutes. Not exactly to everyone's taste, as legendary tough-guy prop-forward, Peter 'Claw' Clohessey, will readily admit.

Those crafty East European sports scientists, however, had taken this whole idea of cold treatment rather more seriously. The Cryo-therapy Unit in Spala was a real chamber of horrors. I arrived a few days after the team, due to the fact that I had a cartilage operation and was still receiving treatment. My first contact with the players was in a mini soccer, volleyball, basketball fun tournament in the camp and I had limped through it with no small pain and effort. The lads then told me I was in for a treat as we were all booked in for a 'cryo' session.

I had no idea what they were talking about but, with great bravado and bluff, appropriate as I thought to a new fitness coach, I laughed all the way to the office where we were kitted out in wooden clogs, knee-length woolen socks, woolen mits, shorts and a surgical mask. This was obviously serious business and doubly so when a doctor monitored my blood pressure.

As I was about to find out, the blood pressure check was to make sure I came out the other side alive and, more importantly, the provision of shorts was to make sure no body parts stuck to the sides of the ice chamber into which I was about to go. Everybody knows that you can easily snap a carrot in half when it is frozen!

About six of us at a time entered the stainless steel cryo chamber, which was like entering a giant freezer, and stood there for an initial one minute. The chamber door was locked shut from the outside by the supervisor and the temperature set at minus 20 degrees! Almost immediately a fog of cold steam made it impossible to see anything and within seconds the hairs on my arms froze white. Seconds more and a deep, creeping iciness spread to the innermost core of my being making me feel like no human can survive more than a few seconds of this. There was still a half minute to go. The lads were laughing and playing survival games, such as name in turn a city beginning with 'M', and if you fail you squat down on hunkers close to the coldest part of the fridge for ten seconds. Thankfully, I came up with a city every time – survival concentrates the mind superbly. Someone de-bagged the diminutive scrumhalf, Peter Stringer, thereby endangering a whole future generation of little Stringers. More raucous laughter. I AM about to die. Then 'DINGG', time up, door opens, stagger out, limbs and joints frozen solid. At least my injured knee doesn't hurt, if it's still there.

Within seconds blood flushes through the whole body and you are totally enveloped in a sense of well-being. That was fun. The next time I am going to enjoy it. By the way, the rush of blood is meant to flush out toxins and aid recovery. Well, no-one ever got to the stage of enjoyment, especially as the timescale was gradually increased to 5 minutes and the temperature to minus 25 degrees. But at least in all the subsequent sessions, and there were two- a- day every day, there was solice in the almost certain knowledge that you were going to come out of the ice box alive.

POLE REUNION

The cryo was memorable; so too was lunch on one occasion. I was standing in the canteen line, tray in hand, when this chap behind me deliberately bumped into me causing my tray to go flying. I turned around, quite annoyed, to see this very familiar face smiling at me. I burst out laughing and we embraced, for it was my old vaulting rival, Polish champion from 1972, Woicek Buciarski. He and his team-mate, Slusarski, had swopped the national record between them until the latter got on top and won the Olympic Gold in Montreal. Woicek was in Spala as the National Athletics Coach for Denmark with a small squad, including his son who was the Danish pole-vault champion. We reminisced over lunch and it was with great sadness that he told me that the former Olympic Champion, Slusarski, had been killed the previous year in a car accident while leaving the Spala camp.

All in all, the trip was very successful, a great opportunity for the 50 best players in the nation to bond away from the pressures of rugby. However, probably the single most influential experience in this respect was the day we all went on a guided tour of Auschwitz. It was harrowing in the extreme, the gas chambers, the ovens, the tons of shorn hair behind a glass partition in one of the barracks, the discarded shoes and prosthetic limbs behind another. That team of young men hardly spoke two words for hours and there were tears in the eyes of some very tough men.

Only a few weeks later there were to be tears in my own eyes and I was left devastated when, following a period of illness (of which I'll talk more later), my irreplaceable wife, Chris, died.

Grand-Slammed

By far the biggest match during my tenure was the 2001 home game to decide the all-conquering England-side's Grand Slam campaign. Lansdowne Road was packed to capacity and Dublin was bursting at its seams with fans from all over the British Isles. The atmosphere was electric. I found it all rather dream-like, but then my psychological state at the time was a bit delicate.

I was still trying to come to terms with the death of my wife, Chris, and had been persuaded by the kindness and warmness of the whole Ireland management team to travel to Dublin and just roll my sleeves up. My daughter Natalie travelled with me and we stayed with the team at the usual Berkeley Court Hotel, beside Lansdowne. The players were marvellous with Natalie, especially after beating England with that famous Keith Wood try and denying them the Grand Slam. We all went out on the town that night as Dublin celebrated long into the wee hours.

Woodie was wonderful both on and off the field of play and quietly and very personally said some beautiful things to myself and to Natalie. He was however subject to the same rules as everyone else in the side. They all had to meet me on the morning after for the stipulated pool recovery session. In my naivety, I had called for all the players to do a short swim session between 9:30 and 10:30am in a near-by pool.

The truth of the matter is I don't think many of the lads got to bed much before 9:30am, so the head count at the poolside was a little sparse. I got there five minutes early, in good time for the half hour planned for stretching and exercising in the water which really helps recovery from all the knocks and bruises of the tough match. Only one player turned up on the dot of 9:30. It was, to my delight, the new wonderkid of Irish rugby, Brian O'Driscoll himself. Even then at that early stage in his career he was showing the kind of professionalism and dedication that was to mark him out as a great player, although I have to say his appreciation of the history of Irish sport fell into question that morning when I was swimming with him in the pool and he asked this still- in-shape old athlete, "Were you a bodybuilder or something, Mike?"

END OF THE LINE

It was late 2001, things had taken this quite shattering change of course since I had become a widower and I was looking to more changes. I decided, after 25 years in the Bangor gym, to sell up. I also resolved to downsize from our large family home which had a no longer necessary three bedrooms and an expansive stretch of garden which contained my late father's little detached bungalow. I set these changes of direction in motion, knowing that things would not happen overnight. The property market was flying high in North Down and I was sure the house, situated within a good area close to the centre of Bangor, would sell quickly. The Gym, however, with my name over the door and all the history entailed, would be a much harder sell. Or so I thought.

In fact, I couldn't have been more wrong. The Gym sale was organized within a few weeks when I was approached by long-term member, old school-days swimming rival and friend, Ian Kirkpatrick, who set the deal up on behalf of son, Paul. Indeed, there were two further offers made at around the same time. No problem. The problem lay in the sale of the house. No firm offers were immediately forthcoming and this led to a further complication. The IRFU at Lansdowne Road made it clear that they expected me, given my newfound freedom of movement, to live in either the Dublin area or in the Munster area of Cork or Limerick. I was prepared to consider the move, if they would give me some time to sell my house first. I was informed in December that I would be expected to move down in January! The Rugby World Cup qualifiers were imminent and the Fitness Coach, me, would be having a very hands-on role in the players' preparation.

Well, this was simply not possible and I must say that I thought that the IRFU's position on this was unsympathetic and unreasonable. They also seemed to be admitting as much when, as soon as I was forced to make the decision to stand down, they agreed to pay my salary for the six months of my contract remaining.

It was at this time that I suddenly, for the first time in my life, free from any professional or sporting commitments, decided to make the long trek South to Spain... and this is, more or less where we came in.

23. Watching the Watcher

The great Zen master Rinzai, in order to take his students' attention away from time, would often raise his finger and slowly ask; "What, at this moment, is lacking?" His answer was, if you are alive to address the question, 'nothing' because being alive in the moment is all that matters.

Target Practice

The trouble with sport, as it is practiced by high level exponents, is that the answer to the master's question would invariably be, 'Everything.' Unless the athlete is actually standing on the victory podium then nothing is complete, everything is lacking. Even then this moment of completeness will be fleeting. There will always be the next championship, the next medal, the next year, the next Olympiad. The athlete's life is firmly fixated on the future. All the training is physical and psychological preparation for an event in the future. A life of sporting excellence is necessarily a life determined by goals and targets. David Hemery in his book, *Sporting Excellence*, says;

> Very high achievers usually have a dream, a hope, even an aim to get to the top. This long-term target is a large motivating factor but along the route there are many smaller targets. Each target can be seen as an end-goal in itself; for example, winning a title, a trophy or promotion. These are not largely in your control, whereas your performance improvement is. Improvement is usually the best route to end-goal success. And there is a process of work of some kind to achieve performance improvement. The attraction of the next-step goal can be a significant motivating factor in the difficult training and preparation times ahead.

This is all very well but when you have been, from an early age, so fundamentally driven by targets and by the eternal quest for achievement, then it becomes a habit; the habit of always looking to the future and to a day when everything will be complete, to some sort of sporting nirvana. The consequence of this way of looking at life, for it soon encompasses all aspects of one's being, is that the present is often lost; the joy of living a life in the Here-and-Now, becomes submerged in this very focussed, target-oriented blueprint of a sporting life.

This unfortunate tendency is exaggerated in the case of Olympic sports persons for whom life is conveniently compartmentalized into 4-year cycles; even more so in individualistic, non-team game types of activities, where the single-minded and often lonely pursuit of training objectives can render everything in the Present purely a means to an end. Everything pales into insignificance when set against the great objective at the end of the next 4-year cycle.

The incomparable David Hemery illustrates this tendency in his book;

> ...I was a student at Boston University. I usually met Billy Smith at 3pm but on this particular day a blizzard had started at noon. I went to the door of the parking area at 3pm not really expecting to see Billy, but instead bumped into him on his way in. I asked whether I should do some weight training or have a day off. He pushed the door open against the wind and driving snow, and said, "Out there's the road to Mexico!"

You see, for an athlete like Hemery or Davies or any of the others with whom I have acquainted you in the foregoing pages, there is always a Mexico out there. There is always an end, a target to aim at, a greater goal. Psychologists call it 'relative deprivation'; the more you deprive yourself of immediate comfort and pleasure, the greater the reward in the long term. Athletes are the masters-of-the-universe of relative deprivation.

Don't misunderstand me, Dave Hemery won the Olympic 400m hurdles Gold by the greatest margin of victory in history in an amazing world record time. He achieved it exactly because of the kind of mutual commitment and respect depicted in this experience with his coach, Billy Smith;

> As I did a series of 800m runs, Billy just stood there with his coat collar up and his back to the wind and driving snow. I hoped that my efforts would raise his respect for me and certainly his presence during the session in those conditions raised mine for him. He had been willing to go through it with me.

ALWAYS SEEKING SOMETHING

Then in the blink of an eye it's all over, the sporting ambition comes to an end. No more convenient 1, 2, 3, or 4-year training plans, no more Grand Designs to give daily life its shape and meaning. But the habits of a lifetime are not easily broken.

What is next? Work hard and complete that research degree; go get that new job; get that business project off the ground; move to that dream house; drive a better car. What about the fading adulation? Recapture some of it with perhaps high profile projects in the media, in politics or in public service. Keep an eye on your social status and public persona and who knows, perhaps a 'gong' will fall your way. And on and on, ad infinitum. This mind-pattern creates an obsession with the future, with attaining goals, with achievement, with looking for something. A life in sport can nourish this obsession. The goal takes up so much of your attention that the present moment is reduced to a means to an end.

There is a lovely story in one of Carl Jung's books where he tells of a conversation with a Native American chief who considered that most white people have 'tense faces' and 'staring eyes.' He said further; "They are always seeking something. What are they seeking? The whites always want something. They are always uneasy and restless. We don't know what they want. We think they are mad."

PROPRIATE STRIVING

Psychologists have again come up with a name for this condition. They call it 'propriate striving'; it is the 'normal' human condition that can be likened to a sort of background static of the mind. There is never any silence, no stillness, no peace, only constant thinking and inner conversation. The only breaks in this internal static come at times of great emotional turmoil, fight, flight, or freeze, life or death, or at times of great physical effort when there is no time for mental rumination and action takes over. At such times it can seem that you are like Adam Smith's 'Impartial Spectator', a detached observer of your own self, watching your self, watching your self think, watching the watcher. You are alert and totally aware of all that is happening. You are very much in the Present.

MIKE BULL - AN OLYMPIAN'S STORY

If sport can predispose you to become obsessed with the future, then the past is the refuge of the retired athlete. Wasn't it Billie Jean King who famously pronounced, "You are only as good as your last performance." The focus shifts to the past. Great victories, achievements and events in your life can become the most prominent features in the background static of the mind. Try writing an autobiography; then you will understand this ever- deepening wallowing in oceans of nostalgia and reminiscence.

COULD HAVE... SHOULD HAVE

When you become fixated on the past there is no conscious present. Many successful sportsmen live in the past. Some make a living out of it. The Present is once again squeezed out of significance. The egocentric mind loves the constant inner chatter of which past sporting glory is a great provider. The mental conversations with your inner voices reach cacophony when you contemplate what you accomplished in the past, what perhaps you might have further achieved, what might have been.

The idea of what might have been has a special place in the chorus of voices heard in the head of the so-called high achiever.

THE LONG BATTLE

In my own case, it is tempting to think that perhaps if I had paid more attention to the Present things might have turned out better. I might have noticed sooner that Chris was losing her long battle with alcohol dependency. You might have thought that the glamour and travel, the acclaim and the status that go hand in hand with sporting success would be a shared experience with your partner, like the garden parties at Buckingham Palace or meeting the Queen aboard the Royal Yacht Britannia. In our case, the visits were shared and the lifestyle but, despite her beauty and style equipping her well for the role, I think that Chris always felt like an outsider.

There is no doubt that Chris found running the women's section of the Gym increasingly stressful and, although she also loved doing it, perhaps the stress was so great that it needed an external panacea. Awareness of the nature of genetic predisposition, of the susceptibility of certain personality types, of the theories of self-destructiveness, doesn't really help when you have been married to someone for 32 years and have been together since you both were teenagers. You may be the last person in the world to realize what is going on.

Chris died on our 32nd wedding anniversary, the 12th of October 2001 due to liver failure. I rushed her to the Ulster Hospital which is only ten minutes from our home. Initially in catastrophic distress, she mercifully fell into a coma from which she never awakened. When Chris took her last breath our two children, Gavin and Natalie, her closest family and friends were right there by her bedside, able to hold her hand.

I had lost forever the beautiful little blonde girl for whom I had returned as a teenager from Southern Illinois University all those years ago. The newspaper story from the *Sunday Life* which followed Chris's funeral was a fitting tribute;

MIKE'S SAD GOODBYE TO LOVING WIFE

ULSTER sporting hero Mike Bull paid a heartbreaking farewell to his biggest supporter – his wife – on an especially poignant day.

For the double Commonwealth Games pole vaulting and decathlon gold medallist said a final goodbye to his loving wife Chris... on their 32nd wedding anniversary.

Close family gathered at the Ulster Hospital in Dundonald as Chris died after a short illness on Friday, October 12th the same date that the couple married at St Gerard's Church in north Belfast back in 1969.

Athletics legend Mike, 54, told Sunday Life: "Chris died on our 32nd wedding anniversary, which was pretty poignant for us. We got married in 1969 with me wearing my Mexico Olympic suit – with badge and blazer. We had been going out together since we were 17. We were both the same age and basically we grew up together and shared all that time. She always came to the sports events with me and we travelled a lot together. All my friends were her friends".

Paying tribute to Chris, he added: "She was very, very shy. She wasn't a pushy person, and was very attractive and always looked so nice". Mike, who made a record 69 appearances in a Great British team vest, added that Chris had been a devoted mother, raising the couple's two children, Gavin and Natalie, at their Bangor home. And in more recent times, the couple continued a winning partnership in the popular Mike Bull Health Studio, based in Bangor.

Mike, who is the Ireland rugby squad's national fitness adviser, revealed that the entire team had attended Chris's funeral in St Comgall's Church, Bangor, earlier this week. "David Humphreys helped to carry the coffin, as did three of the other Ireland lads – prop Justin Fitzpatrick, centre Jonathan Bell and Ulster captain Andy Ward. I couldn't believe it. It was such a lovely tribute." Other friends who paid their respects included Irish rugby fitness director Liam Hennessey, and 1964 Olympic long jump gold medallist Lynn Davies and his wife Meriel.

CARESSING THE WEIGHTS

Watching the watcher is really a nifty sort of linguistic trick, a logical impossibility whenever it is self-referring. That is to say, it is not possible to watch yourself watching (outside of film, mirrors or out-of-the-body experiences). Our ordinary language solves this problem by making 'watching' a sort of mental activity; (see P. F. Strawson's landmark 'Persons' if you want to pursue this issue). It is really a way of describing an aspirational ability that everyone can activate by learning to make a little place in a busy life for some sort of meditation. Meditation, if I have understood the great spiritual teachers, is not the same as thought; it is, in fact, the state of non-thought, of stillness. Paradoxically, sport and physical exercise are a good medium for this strange sort of stillness. Not the target-obsessed process of high achievement, but rather the displacement sort of activity that is not of itself goal-directed; as 84 year-old bodybuilder Eric Dowey would say back in the days of the Bangor gym, "Do it because you love doing it – caress the weight as you set it down." I hoped to find a little piece of this stillness in southern Spain. Of course, as I have already intimated, the most incompatible thing in the world to achieving some sort of mental calm is the act of writing an autobiography. However, a life in sport has at least prepared me well for the activity of writing, the daily work routine, the self-discipline, the intense focus on the end product. Now that it is done, perhaps there is more room for the Here and Now.

24. THE POWER OF FOUR

Dating from the period 2003 to date, four life-altering events have taken place.

THE FIRST – LYNDA

I was back in Bangor, Co. Down, in 2005, working away at my little personal training project at the Marine Court Hotel, just making ends meet. I had bunked in with my old friend and gym employee, the now very successful businessman, Alan Nappin, so overheads were low.

Lynda

One of those days when the gods were smiling, I was training in the hotel gym and was approached by a stunning young female athlete who asked if she could hire me professionally to train her and thus I met Lynda.

I agreed, of course, and thereby does a man change the course of his life. We found we had a lot in common, she a recent widow and me a widower, both mad keen on training and sports, and roughly the same age (give or take 17 years)? Before going into any details in trying to describe Lynda, I give way to a striking resemblance described in an excellent, newish book by film star Tom Hanks (this is a tactic to spare

Lynda's blushes). This book of short stories is called *Uncommon Type* and the first chapter is a story about the narrator's meeting and falling for a dark-haired beauty who is Lynda to a tee!

All the physical similarities are there, the mane of jet-black hair, dark, sultry Spanish good looks, film-star smile to light up any room, the athlete's physique framed by rope-like musculature combined with feminine curves. As Hanks described it, this woman's physical attributes were only part of the package, the other parts were even more fascinating!

Like Lynda, she, I recall that her name was Anna, was highly educated with a razor-sharp brain and with a master's degree which, in Lynda's case, was in Physical Activity and Population Health. They both ran their own companies and held down high-powered jobs, displaying boundless energy and enthusiasm over a wide range of professional and social and sporting interests. The interesting bit though, is that all this whirlwind activity is done without the need for much sleep, or relaxation, or food!

Anna would go to bed at a normal hour, maybe sleep for a couple of hours, get up in the middle of the night and rearrange the furniture, paint the kitchen ceiling, do a bit of work on the computer and then go for a 10k run, shower, hair and make-up, bake multi-seeded scones for breakfast, and then wake her slumbering paramour with a kiss before flying out of the door to the first appointment of the day.

Lynda would do all of that and more. Once upon a time, at my Spanish apartment, I awoke in the morning to find that the terrace tiles had been painted a shining white, and that a professional-looking architect's plan had been drawn up to knock down a wall and create a new, space-saving galley kitchen. I looked around to express my delight to Lynda but, alas, she had gone for a 10k run along the paseo maritimo.

When I first met her, Lynda was an accomplished yachtswoman, owning and sailing solo, her own 54ft Amel ketch out of Bangor Marina. She taught me the ropes and eventually I learned enough to crew with her in the Caribbean, race in the British Virgin Islands, and, the final accolade, to be her 'galley slave' aboard the 'Vic 32', the legendary Clyde Puffer steamboat which had been adapted to the Scottish tourist industry. We had many adventures over a four-year period, cooking and cleaning, singing and dancing, with skipper Nick Walker at the helm. Lynda, as if cooking three meals and two collations (freshly baked scones and fruitcake) as well as helping out at the helm and operating the lough gates of the Crinan and Caledonian canals) was so inspired by the local Scottish folk musicians all around the Western Isles that she learned to play the flute!

Along the way, Lynda and I had been running 10k's and cycling 80 miles and swimming, once entering the 2-mile sea swim around Goat Island, beside Corfu. She finished second in that race – I was first; well, I had to beat her at something! There were to be precious few opportunities to keep up with her relentless schedule in the coming years, four marathons and triathlons under her belt so far.

Tom Hanks's Anna, having lived very happily and excitingly with her older, male companion for several years, one day spontaneously suggested to him that things weren't working out. He had likewise been agonizing over how to tell Anna that he was totally exhausted and needed a break. They agreed to break. However, as the subsequent chapters of Uncommon Type reveal, they remained the best of friends, seeing each other regularly and going on to many adventures together. Back in the real world, you could say that real life imitates art.

THE SECOND - THE LONDON OLYMPICS AND THE OBE

It was May 2012, and I had just returned to Lynda's house from the gym to find her in the kitchen with a mischievous look on her face and a badly disguised 'everything as normal' attitude; "Some mail for you on the table" she suggested, airily I thought.

On top of the pile of boring bills was a smallish, beige envelope embossed with the Royal Seal. Interesting! I opened it carefully and saw that it was from the Cabinet Office. Exciting! The text informed me that the Queen would be offering me the award of 'Officer Of The Order Of The British Empire' in her forthcoming Jubilee Birthday Honours List and asked whether or not I would accept the honour. I would, and with Lynda watching me reading this as if she already knew something (she did know something and had been colluding with the Government on the matter!), we hugged each other in a hysterical fit of tears and laughter.

We danced around the kitchen, shouting inanities and laughing, finally settling down to read the fine print. I had been awarded an OBE for services to sport and charity and, the most difficult part of all, we were to keep it a secret until Her Majesty announced the full list on her birthday, June 16th, some six weeks away! A very frustrating proposition when all you want to do is go out and shout the good news to everyone.

The Investiture itself at Buckingham Palace was to take place on the 13th of December, an interminable six months away. What to do to in the interim to maintain control and manage this secret, life-altering turn of events? I suggested we should throw a party for all our family and friends. I was only moderately surprised to learn that Lynda had already drawn up a provisional list of guests and created a sumptuous lunch menu and had secured a suitable venue and date for our celebration party. June 16th it was to be, the Queen's birthday and day of the

Mary and I in our 'glad rags'
Declan Roughan

Press release, with the Royal Ulster Yacht Club as the fitting venue (we were both members).

The party was fantastic, lots of wine and a huge fresh salmon platter preoccupying the 50 guests, with a brilliant one-man-band, in the form of Lynda's music teacher Alan Crawford, providing the entertainment. The star guests included Dame Mary Peters (now Lady Mary of course), my old pole-vaulting friend and mentor David Stevenson, CBE, his wife Alix, who herself was an Olympic long jumper, and Lady Karen Girvan, MBE, who was, with me, co-founder of SPARKS Northern Ireland. Lynn Davies sent a telegram explaining that he couldn't make it due to the fact that David Stevenson had been unable to land his private Citation Jet at Marshfield, near Cardiff, to pick him up en route to Belfast! Furthermore, did David forget that he was an Olympic Champion and the President of UK Athletics, and that his own daughter had been named Lynn after him?

I am only half joking here, the part about David and Alix flying in on a private jet is true. When I was telling this story at my party speech, Mary, who made a typically brilliant speech herself, laughed loudly and knowingly. She knew Lynn so well as a team-mate, a co-manager of the British Olympic Athletic team and friend, that the whole story could have been true. During Lynn's 10-year presidential reign he had developed a penchant for prefacing his discussions with me about everything, what Spanish bar to frequent, what to have for dinner, what training session we should do, any topic whatever with, "Don't you realize I am President?"

Buckingham Palace was my personal flight into space. On December 13th, 2012, Lynda, son Gavin and daughter Natalie accompanied me on this interstellar journey. The weather was ice-cold, crisply sunny and windless, so all the tails, tall hats and fine lace were securely in place (and that was only the men!) when we entered the Mall. It was a dreamlike experience strolling through the historic Palace, with the art galleries, the elegant rooms and the sense of occasion.

On the command, I stepped forward, bowed my head and received the award of OBE from Prince Charles. We chatted briefly, recalling the several times we had met before, sometimes in the company of his mother

Receiving the OBE from Prince Charles at the 2012 investiture

The Power of four: L-R Gavin, Lynda, me, Natalie

and father, usually at a garden party or athletics reception. I was very impressed that he actually remembered.

Lynda, Natalie and Gavin, who were in the gallery only a few yards away, noticed that the Prince's equerry seemed to be making eye contact with either of the two girls, or possibly both. I was oblivious to all this while chatting to the Prince, but a short time later when the formalities had been completed, the equerry approached Gavin and a grand reunion of old mates occurred. They had been colleagues in the RAF together! Lynda and Natalie did a good job of pretending not to be disappointed at the object of the handsome officer's interest! It certainly turned out to be a day to remember for all of us.

Final note, I got a congratulatory text from Linda McAuley, Tom's well known BBC presenter daughter, Tom being the same man who got the shipyard training base for me back in 1968 and together with my father built the wooden run-up and landing area which propelled me into world-class vaulting. It said, '*Tom McAuley and John Bull will be sharing a wee toast in Heaven today. Congratulations Mike!*'

Many other messages, including from Meriel and Lynn, shared the same sentiment. You cannot harbor any regrets about things like this but if my father had witnessed that medal being pinned on his son's chest at Buckingham Palace, there would have been one very proud Englishman that fine day.

THIRD – THE GREATEST EVER

That was the year of the London Olympics, 2012, and that was to be the occasion of a grand reunion with David Stevenson, my old teammate

THE POWER OF FOUR

and friend, now a happily retired philanthropist. He and Alix and Lynda and I had gone to a Royal Albert Hall fund-raising concert in aid of the Olympic Appeal. It was a brilliant concert, hosted by and starring Gary Barlow OBE of 'Take That' fame. The evening climaxed with an auction, during which I kept my head down to exclude myself from the thousands of pounds being bid for the items. Not so David, bidding successfully for a batch of Olympic Athletics tickets at around £15,000. He had to spend the money, he explained in his best Scottish accountant persona, because of tax reasons. Canny as ever!

I was to be the recipient of one of the coveted tickets, so we next met up on the appointed day of the pole-vault final at the Olympic Stadium. It was a fantastic competition, with France's Lavillenie winning with 5.98m and Gt. Britain's Steve Lewis finishing a terrific equal 5th. The stadium was packed to its 40,000 capacity when David and I grabbed a refreshment on the concourse, I am paying for the beer in my usual generous way (the price printed on the ticket given to me by David was a cool £750!). As I turned to give David his beer, a familiar figure brushed past us talking animatedly on his mobile. It was Mr. Pole-Vault himself, Sergey Bubka, still world record-holder, six-time world champion and former Olympic Champion. Now in his fifties, he looked much the same as his imperious best and I thought he might say hello to two old Olympic vaulters. So, I approached him, introducing us as 1964, in David's case, and 1968 and 1972 in mine, Olympic vaulters. Sergey thrust out a firm handshake, saying, "Mike, David, great to meet you!"

BULL CHARGES TO TOP OF ALL-TIME LIST

By GERRY CARSON

ATHLETICS

NORTHERN Ireland pole vault legend Mike Bull is joint top in a ranking list of the UK's all time best performers compiled by Mel Watman, one of the world's most respected athletics statisticians.

Featured in the magazine Athletics Weekly, Mel's rankings, using a points system to evaluate performances, has Mike and Geoff Elliot as equal first in lists which used heights cleared from the 1930s up to the present day.

Mike, who recently turned 69, still holds the Northern Ireland record with his best clearance of 5.25m set 42 years ago at London's Crystal Palace Stadium.

In a long and distinguished career Bull is the only athlete to win gold medals at both the pole vault and decathlon at the Commonwealth Games, in Edinburgh in 1970 and in Christchurch in 1974.

He set 10 UK national records, first with 4.72m in 1966 and ending with that 5.25m performance.
● THE death of renowned coach Sean Kyle has been mourned throughout Ireland and beyond. The man who inspired countless internationals and one of the founders of Ballymena AC and the now long gone All-Ireland Bears' Club is a sad loss to sport. Condolences go to his wife Maeve and family especially from all who benefited from his skill and advice.

LEADING MAN: Mike Bull

and immediately turning on his heels to resume his mobile conversation, no doubt plotting some momentous political manoeuvre in his quest to head world athletics. We chuckled knowingly, like the two old farts in The Bucket List, and went happily back to our seats.

After all the Olympic fanfare had died down and life resumed its normal routine, I received a timely morale boost in the form of a much-heralded analytical report into finding Britain's Greatest-Ever exponents of their respective events. The analysis was conducted by the world-leading athletics statistician, Mel Watman, and published in October 2015 in the national magazine, Athletics Weekly. Based on an objective points system employed by statisticians, I was Number One! The Greatest Ever British pole-vaulter, an honour to be shared with the late, great Geoff Elliott who performed in the metal pole era of the fifties. When all is said and done, to be so judged in the sport that you have devoted most of your life to, is very special. If the OBE was about a life lived inside sport and extending beyond, then 'The Greatest' was a precise, purist recognition of sporting achievement. Enough said.

FOURTH - IMMORTALITY

When Professor Alistair Macintyre was appointed as the external examiner for my PhD thesis at Queen's University Belfast, I was mightily impressed (and terrified) that Prof Alan Milne, my doctoral supervisor, had secured such an eminent British philosopher to review my humble research. The truth was, they were old student friends from days long past. On the appointed day of the viva ordeal, in Alan's office, he asked his old friend, "What's this new book of yours going to be about, Alistair?" He replied, "Oh, just the usual stuff Alan, God, Freedom and Immortality!"

As they were both Humanists, the God part of the question would no doubt be settled. Their Libertarian leanings would doubtless support the concept of Freedom in its various guises. On Immortality, I timidly proffered my own thoughts that it really only had meaning in the context of 'the immortal gene'.

The illustrious professors have left the stage now, but I now have more evidence to support my position on this, in the form of my children and their families.

Gavin became an air-traffic controller in the RAF and is currently successfully doing the same, but now in civy-street in London. At school Gavin excelled at football, tennis and golf and was a willing and talented instructor at our gym before embarking on his military career. That special father/son bond was forged by all this activity and continues to this day, although now it's a case

Gavin

of me bunking in his spare room in London on my frequent, pre-pandemic trips to the mainland. He has a teenage son, Adam (16 years), who is arguably a better footballer than his Dad (I'm really in trouble now), but not as good a cyclist (safer ground). It has been nostalgic in recent times, when Adam's successful junior football team in Newry wasn't able to train together to get regular texts "Grandpa Mike, I'm bored with the weights programme you gave me last month, can you give me a new one?" Like father, like son!

Adam

Natalie's sporting prowess is well documented, her school days gymnastic ability giving way to success in triathlon and ironman, finishing 17th in the World Half Ironman Championships in Austria a couple of years ago. She initially started out in a career as a sports therapist before

Max

Natalie

undertaking a career change with a new degree in Leadership and Management from Dundee. She has two footballer sons, Bangor's Max Davidson (18 years), and Ballymena's Ben (15 years) who like Adam get their training programmes regularly updated by the 'old man'.

Ben

When I watch my grandsons training and playing football, I sometimes see reflections of that St Malachy's schoolboy who had dreams and passion for a somewhat more esoteric sporting activity. That immortal gene lives on.

ACKNOWLEDGEMENTS

This book has been a long time in the making and I have to thank a cast of hundreds who have encouraged me over the years of writing in order to get to this point. An appropriate place to start is with my daughter, Natalie Bull-Davidson, who hunted down the long-time lost original, manually typed manuscript which had been lost for many years. Without her all these words would have been lost forever.

Then there was a wee bit of technological wizardry from fellow gym members, John and Anita Wyers. Anita took the scrappy old pages of the original script to her workplace where a colleague converted them, by virtue of some computer magic, into a workable Word format that I could edit and rewrite to my heart's content. Thanks also to Kimberly at Bangor Colour Print for turning it into a legible manuscript.

The original story was mostly recast and what with the constant encouragement of Lynda Fielden, Lynn Davies and Lady Mary, to name a few, it was, I hope, made into a better read.

Fellow writer and journalist, Maurice Neill, also hectored me to "keep on going, you can get a deal!" But writing was always easier than publishing. Quite a coven of publishers showed interest and things looked promising…then there was Covid and all bets were off; that is until I met up with Tim Johnston of Ballyhay Books. Tim liked what he saw and not only did he roll the dice, he marked them. He called it as he saw it, "Hmmm… the first chapter's crap… have another go and rewrite it with something that grabs me and makes me want to read on." He was spot on and I liked the attitude. In sport, a good coach has to be honest and direct. Tim was that, "…bombs and bullets are the backdrop, not the story" Right again! "And give me more anecdotes. We all love the insider's story." Well, I have tried.

As for the book's title, I had all sorts of cryptic, philosophical allusions lined up. "Keep it simple." was Tim's plea, and so Lynda came up with *Mike Bull, An Olympian's Story*. Pragmatic as ever, thanks Lynda.

Thanks to Lynn Davies CBE for his kind foreword. That will cost me a few wee drams in our local tavern.

EPILOGUE:
ICARUS FLIES AGAIN

Pushing up the average age: L-R Jim Alexander, (head coach), Pete Glass, Abbie O'Neill, me, Erin Fisher, Dr Lynne Fisher

If the Hemmingway complex wears off and the writing dries up then there is always the old stand-by; I could always start vaulting again. Last year, 2020, the brilliantly knowledgeable and tireless (OK, I'm crawling!) N. Ireland National Pole Vault Coach, Jim Alexander (I believe in collusion with UK pole vault coach, six times World Masters Champion and old team mate of mine, Allan Williams), asked me if I fancied coming over to one of the jump sessions he was organizing. I went over to watch but ended up having a go (Jim knows me so well, he knew I wouldn't be able to resist even if my wings had melted a little). Anyway, despite knee cartilage operations and a few hospital visits, I found I could still vault. At least my brain knew exactly what to do, even though the flesh was a bit wanting. As George Best had said to me during one of those Superstars events in the 1980's, "Mike, I know where I want to go with the ball, but my feet are a yard behind!"

Having said that I've been able to keep in good physical condition at the gym at Bangor's Marine Court Hourt Hotel (when it was owned by my in-laws, the Diamonds) and more recently at the town's Aurora Centre... so I'm still having a go at the grand old age of 74!

In the inspiring company of the elite vault squad members, Pete Glass, Abbie O'Neill, Erin Fisher, Jamie, Owen, Troy, Finlay and new young star Ellie who have all been warned by coaches Williams and Alexander not to damage the 'National Treasure'. They make me feel like one of Buster's delicate and priceless Ming Dynasty Gongs but in spite of that I've found it, and all the weight-training, running and sprinting that you have to do just to get airborne, a great panacea to the ongoing pandemic. Given another few years or so I could end up, if not exactly the last man standing, then one of the last men vaulting. A good epitaph!

Dear Reader,

I hope you have enjoyed this publication from Ballyhay Books, an imprint of Laurel Cottage Ltd. We publish an eclectic mix of books ranging from personal memoirs to authoritative books on local history, from sport to poultry, from photographs to fiction and from music to marine interests – but all with a distinctly local flavour.

To see details of these books, as well as the beautifully illustrated books of our sister imprint Cottage Publications, why not visit our website **www.cottage-publications.com** or telephone +44 (0)28 9188 8033.

Timothy S Johnston

BALLYHAY BOOKS